WILLIAM JAMES
ON
EXCEPTIONAL MENTAL
STATES

WILLIAM JAMES

on Exceptional Mental States
The 1896 Lowell Lectures

EUGENE TAYLOR

The University of Massachusetts Press
Amherst, 1984

First published in 1983 by Charles Scribner's Sons
and reprinted by their permission
Library of Congress Cataloging in Publication Data
Taylor, Eugene.
William James on exceptional mental states.
Includes bibliographical references and index.
1. Personality—Addresses, essays, lectures.
2. Subconsciousness—Addresses, essays, lectures.
3. Psychology, Pathological—Addresses, essays, lectures.
4. James, William, 1842–1910—Addresses, essays,
lectures. I. Title.
BF698. T 39   616.89   83-9079
ISBN 0-87023-451-X
Quotations from the James Papers are used by permission
of Mr. Alexander R. James and the Houghton Library,
Harvard University.

In honor of the
Alexander R. James Family
of
Dublin, New Hampshire

CONTENTS

PREFACE AND
ACKNOWLEDGMENTS

The reconstruction of William James's unpublished Lowell Lectures on Exceptional Mental States began early in 1977 with a number of significant and simultaneous discoveries. First, James's original handwritten lecture notes were found among the James Papers in the Houghton Rare Manuscript Library at Harvard; second, related correspondence and lecture announcements were discovered in the same library among the Lowell Institute Papers. Then, a close examination of the literary sources detailed in the lecture notes led to the discovery of some 936 volumes from James's family library, given to Harvard by his heirs in 1923 upon the death of his wife, Alice Gibbens James. These books and pamphlets were deposited throughout the open stacks of Harvard's 3-million-volume Widener Collection, where they remained safely housed but scattered for more than fifty years.

With the help of graduate students from Harvard Divinity School, Loretta Czernis, Lauri Teidie, and Deborah Graves, the bibliographic skills of Mrs. Wilfred Cantwell Smith, and a research grant from the Cabot Fund, I conducted a search of the Widener Collection to find these books. They amounted to some seventy-five shelf feet, most of them dealing with topics in abnormal psychology, psychical research, "demon possession," and psychology of religion. Many were source books for James's *Varieties of Religious Experience* (1902). In addition, many books and pamphlets belonged to what William's son Henry James, the lawyer, called one of the largest collections ever assembled of crank literature from New England at the turn of the century. "Ephemeral," he termed them, for they could hardly be replaced, and they are important when taken as a whole.

Once the search had been completed, more than 200 of the 936 items were found to contain some combination of James's signature, marginal marks, and penciled index on the last blank page. Some had letters inserted between the pages. In these two hundred are occasional marks or brief annotations, as well as page references keyed to James's unpublished 1896 Lowell Lectures, a connection consistently overlooked by previous James scholars. Once located, all marked or annotated volumes were transferred to the Houghton Library, where other books marked by James have been on deposit since 1923.

A word is perhaps appropriate here concerning James's system of annotation. In order to peruse a vast literature on a variety of subjects in at least four languages, James early adopted the habit of speed reading. He would run rapidly through an entire volume, marking as he went passages of interest with a single stroke—an artist's line, always in pencil, always with the same pressure. Only in volumes of the greatest interest or most frequent use for some particular project did he write in the margins. Otherwise, he most often made notes in the penciled index he would draw up in the last few blank pages of the book.

A particular volume, rich in clues, might contain James's signature, address, a signature or letter from the author, marginal markings, page references in the margins referring to other pages in the book, and copious entries in the penciled index in the back. A bookplate on the inside front cover pasted in by the Harvard Library in 1923 would show that the volume came from the James library. In other cases the clues might be scant. There might be only the bookplate and a single faint pencil line on only one page in the entire book. Yet that single line would take on significance if the idea it signalized, along with the author's name and a page number, appeared in the notes for the Exceptional Mental States Lectures.

The James family recognized these markings as important when they made their gift to Harvard in 1923. Abraham Aaron Roback, the psychologist and Yiddish scholar who was involved in transfer of the gift, also acknowledged their importance when in 1946 he published a preliminary analysis of James's system of annotation in *William James: His Marginalia, Personality, and Contribution,* as have a handful of other scholars over the years. But a rich field for investigation still remains.

These discoveries led in turn to other collections, chief among which was the discovery of Henry James, Sr.'s, extensively annotated set of works by Emanuel Swedenborg. They reposed in the legendary trunk that Henry James the novelist described as the one permanent fixture during the family's European travels. The ideas that it contained, he said, loomed large in his own early career. The trunk and its contents, inherited by William James upon his father's death, were given to the Swedenborg School of Religion in Newton, Massachusetts, by the James Estate in the early 1960s. The collection has since been enlarged by the addition of copies of previously unavailable letters written in the 1840s and 1850s between Henry James, Sr., and James John Garth Wilkinson, English physician and translator of Swedenborg, who was a friend of Thomas Carlyle and Ralph Waldo Emerson. Taken collectively, these materials shed new light on some of the Swedenborgian and Transcendentalist roots of ideas that William James developed in his later career. New perspectives are thereby suggested for the influence of the family literary legacy on William's subsequent interest in mental therapeutics. At the same time the documents reveal the influence of Henry James, Sr.'s, interpretation of Swedenborg on C. S. Peirce's doctrine of pragmatism in the 1860s and on Peirce's cosmology in the 1890s. The logical inference from this is that William James subsequently adopted certain of his father's ideas through Peirce's writings.

Another discovery was the Harvard Library Charging Records, housed in the University Archives, which showed the volumes James checked out of the college between 1861, the year he entered the Lawrence Scientific School, and 1896, when a different method of recording charges was adopted. In order to understand these records, the history of the library's many classification systems had to be reconstructed. This was undertaken in the summer of 1979 by Dr. Thomas Cadwallader from Indiana State University and William Whalen, assistant at the Harvard Archives, and completed in 1981 by Jennifer Zukowski and myself. Books and pamphlets from these Charging Records that pertain to the Exceptional Mental States Lectures were then traced to the library shelves and many were found to contain annotations by James in a form identical to those he used in his own books.

The greatest number of charges was recorded between 1889 and 1896, during which time James was a full professor of psychology (1889–98) and taught, in addition to introductory courses in philosophy and psychology, graduate seminars in mental pathology (1892–98), or what we would now call today abnormal psychology.

The actual dates and times of the lectures were established through tickets and brochures found among the Lowell Institute Papers. Then, with the help of Gabriel Palmer-Fernandez, a search was made at the Boston Public Library of local newspapers from the fall of 1896. Accounts of six of the eight talks were located, in addition to two major summaries of the entire series. There is one clue suggesting that

James may have contributed to the newspaper releases himself; at any rate, some of the accounts contain long verbatim quotations corresponding exactly to the progression of the lecture notes.

I am particularly indebted to Professor William Rogers of the Department of Applied Theology, Harvard Divinity School, and Professor Sheldon White of the Harvard Department of Psychology and Social Relations for acting as faculty advisers to the project; acknowledgments are extended also to the Cabot Fund for the archival research grant that originally launched my undertaking; and to Dr. and Mrs. Henry A. Murray, Mr. and Mrs. Mario Nicosia, and Professor Frank Davidson for continued financial support. Thanks are due, in addition, to the circulation staff of Widener Library for their tireless aid in searching for lost books, especially John Lanham, Frank Cox, and Edward Doctoroff; to Charles Montalbano of the Widener Stack Division; to the reference department of Widener Library and the reading room staff of Houghton Library; and to the staff of the Harvard University Archives, especially Clark Eliot, assistant curator, who first drew my attention to the library Charging Records. Thanks are also due to Annalise Katz of the Harvard Psychology Library. To Richard Wolfe, curator of rare books and manuscripts at the Harvard Medical School and librarian of the Boston Medical Library, who continuously gave far-reaching support, I owe a special debt.

Marguerite Levine, archivist of the Helen Keller Papers at the American Foundation for the Blind in New York, and Bernadette Perrault of the Harvard Divinity Library staff supplied translations from James's French sources; Silvia Marinara helped with James's Italian case studies; while Christian Mañia and especially Marianne Teuber amazed me with their German translations. To Geraldine Stevens I owe a great debt for her extensive editorial advice during the preliminary stages of composition; Lawrence Levine,

Jack Roy Strange, and Eugene I. Taylor, Sr., read the manuscript for errors; June Doezema and Gary Bisbee gave typing assistance, and Jean Michener typed the finished copy.

Finally, I must thank Alexander R. James, current literary executor of the James Estate, for permission to publish unpublished James material in its presently reconstructed form; Roger Stoddard of Houghton Library for permission to consult James's original lecture notes; John Lowell for permission to reproduce material from the Lowell Institute Papers; and Dr. Jacques Barzun for his editorial efforts at Charles Scribner's Sons.

A final note is needed about the form in which the lectures have been cast. Any word, phrase, sentence, or paragraph found within quotation marks is William James speaking, even if only a fragment is quoted. Where appropriate, these quotations are supplied with a reference and their source is given. If unreferenced, the quotations in almost every case come from James's original notes. Any sentence or passage found without quotation marks is my own completion of a thought, usually derived from some abbreviation in James. Quotation marks have been eliminated around some single words that appear in James's notes because the words are of common usage and the elimination of the quotation marks improved the flow of the text. In these cases the common words still conform to James's original notes.

The use of quotation marks in this manner was adopted to create an unobstructed text for the reader and still keep intact what James actually said. It also allowed occasional digressions from the text for brief comment. Such a format evolved from the redelivery of the Exceptional Mental States series in 1978–79 for the Cambridge Swedenborg Society, in cooperation with the Swedenborg School of Religion and the Department of Applied Theology at Harvard Divinity School. The series was then given as a one-lecture summary before the clinical psychology colloquium at Yale University, thanks to the kindness of Dr. Jerome Singer. The historical introduction was delivered in December 1981 as an address in the medical humanities program, Department of Psychiatry, Harvard Medical School, under the auspices of Drs. Charles Ducey and Bennet Simon.

EUGENE TAYLOR
Cambridge, Massachusetts
August 13, 1982

WILLIAM JAMES
ON
EXCEPTIONAL MENTAL
STATES

HISTORICAL
INTRODUCTION

William James advocated a balance between science and religion in an age when religious themes had been plowed under and the scientific outlook had just begun its meteoric rise within American culture. He spoke out against the Social Darwinists by supporting the supremacy of individual choice in mental, as opposed to a strictly biological, evolution; he attacked medical materialism by emphasizing the healing power of personal religious experience; and he argued against the supremacy of the intellect by stressing the primacy of emotions, the importance of our sentiments, and the efficacy of our beliefs in his total view of human personality. William James became the champion of eclecticism and open-mindedness in an age of increasing narrowness and specialization.

Prior to 1890, James had involved himself with the new scientific psychology—the so-called experimental psychology of the subconscious emerging in France and the physiological laboratory tradition of the German universities. This he tempered with moral guidance from the British philosophers and the skepticism, advanced by English savants in psychical research, of rational science and reasonable religion. But psychology for James was not simply a subset of philosophy;

he argued for its recognition as a distinct empirical discipline, both cognitive and positivistic in orientation. This was the view he took in his famous *Principles of Psychology* in 1890. Yet, after 1890, James had a turn of mind. Increasingly disenchanted with a scientific psychology in America that restricted itself more and more to the laboratory and to the filtering of reality through a clouded lens of statistical analysis, James sought to extend the discipline by including within it the study of psychic phenomena, the subconscious, and religious experience. He hoped less to make such explorations scientifically respectable than to use them as a means for transforming the ever-narrowing definition of science itself.

James was particularly aided in this effort by the fact that New England in the 1890s was a veritable caldron of ideas— swirling cross-currents of new experiments in medicine, psychotherapy, and mental healing. It was the *Zeitgeist* of this era that he attempted to capture in 1896 with the presentation of his Lowell Lectures on Exceptional Mental States.

HISTORICAL BACKGROUND OF THE TALKS

In the decades preceding the 1896 lectures, James had maintained an abiding interest in the relationship of psychotherapy to mental healing. This interest was in part a legacy of his family's relationship to James John Garth Wilkinson, homeopathic physician and translator of Swedenborg's pre-theological works, and to the New England Transcendentalists; in part a function of James's personal search for a workable solution to his own emotional and physical difficulties; and in part due to the blossoming of the mental healing movement from the 1840s onward in New England, especially in Boston. James had been involved with the American branch of the English Society for Psychical Research and their efforts to test scientifically the claims of the mental healers since the early 1880s. He had published articles on mental pathology in various journals and in his *Principles,* and had been investigating the moral causes of illness from the time he had decided on a medical degree in the early 1860s. Going before the Massachusetts Legislature in 1894, and again in 1898, James pleaded eloquently and successfully in defense of the mental healers, protecting them against attacks by the medical profession.

In 1893–94 he taught at Harvard his first psychological seminary on mental pathology, which he gave again every year until 1898. The year James delivered his Lowell Lectures, he also taught this graduate course in abnormal psychology, using Henry Maudsley's *Pathology of Mind* (1867) as his text. Throughout, he had been attending international conferences, keeping abreast of the newest advances in psychotherapeutics, and writing extensive reviews of developments in psychotherapy coming from England, France, Germany, and Italy; with his students he had been visiting various asylums in Massachusetts; and on occasion he had traveled to the Worcester State Hospital with his private physician and friend, James Jackson Putnam, to consult with the famous Swiss psychiatrist Adolf Meyer.[1]

There is even some evidence to suggest that James took several patients suffering from functional disturbances into his own home, treating at least one of them successfully with hypnosis and suggestion.[2] From all these activities there grew what later came to be known as the Boston School of Psychotherapy (or the School of Abnormal Psychology), a loose-knit group of professionals who were pioneers in treating mental diseases that had no organic basis. These innovators helped to create the climate for the introduction of Freud and psychoanalysis to America before 1909.[3]

THE LOWELL SETTING

Under the sponsorship of one of Boston's wealthiest families, the Lowell Institute had been offering public lectures since its founding in 1836 for the purpose of providing the city's general population with exposure to the most eminent scholars of the time. Although the lectures were open gratis to the public, the speakers were paid handsomely for the delivery of a single series. In the Institute's history, such luminaries as C. Lloyd Morgan, Edward Everett Hale, James Russell Lowell, Jared Sparks, Asa Gray, Louis Agassiz, Oliver Wendell Holmes, Josiah Royce, Francis Greenwood Peabody, and Charles Sanders Peirce had spoken, as did Charles Rockwell Lanman, Pierre Janet, and Theodore Roosevelt later. James's was the second course of the 1896–97 season, preceded by Dr. Louis C. Elson from the Conservatory of Music, who spoke on "Symphony and Orchestra," and followed by six lectures on "The Religion of Primitive People" by Dr. Dan Brinton of the University of Pennsylvania.[4]

In addition to teaching his regular classes at Harvard, James began his lectures for the Lowell Institute in October at Huntington Hall in the Back Bay area of Boston. They were held on successive Wednesday and Saturday evenings. October 21, 24, 28, 31, and November 4, 7, 11, and 14, beginning promptly at 7:45 P.M. and lasting approximately one hour. Admission was by pre-mailed ticket. According to the Institute's account of the ticket returns, there was an initial crush of several hundred that tapered off to a more stable 100 to 150 as the lectures proceeded. James, however, wrote that the hall was filled to the end of the series. While the newspaper accounts were sometimes detailed and lively, the only entry in the "Janitor's Notebook" was: "second course of eight lectures by Professor William James, M.D. etc. (Harvard) on the Exceptional Mental States (rather dry)."[5]

James first proposed his series in a letter to Augustus

Lowell dated April 18, 1896. He said: "I wrote to you some six weeks ago with reference to Mr. C. H. Hinton of Princeton as a possible Lowell lecturer. I am now taking the liberty of annoying you in a similar way with regard to another candidate, namely *myself.*" What he offered was: "a mass of floating matter that is hardly yet codified and organized, but that is becoming more and more so, and that has great practical and historical importance, to which for some years past I have been giving a good deal of attention, and which I think I could bring together in an instructive way."[6] He then listed ten subjects—later shortened to eight, namely: "Dreams and Hypnotism," "Automatism," "Hysteria," "Multiple Personality," "Demoniacal Possession," "Witchcraft," "Degeneration," and "Genius."

The purpose of the lectures, James subsequently wrote to a friend, was to avoid psychic or occult themes, and, instead, to bring together the newest insights in the field of suggestive therapeutics with those from psychotherapy, medicine, and psychology. He intended to deal with decidedly morbid subjects, but wished to "shape our thoughts about them toward optimistic and hygienic conclusions."[7] Too long had morbidity been treated as something fixed, unalterable, and somehow different from the normal. Long before Freud, it was James who had said that we are of one clay with lunatics and criminals. His import was to destroy our view of untouchability surrounding the insane. In the end, however, lest he should disappoint his hearers, he could not resist making frequent allusions to the occult.

PRIMARY THEMES OF EACH LECTURE

In organizing the lectures, James changed his mind three times. His first selection of ten topics had been reduced to eight by the time the tickets were printed, but he switched the order of Lectures II and III when actually delivering them. This is corroborated both by newspaper accounts giving the progression of each talk and by the order and page numbering of the original lecture notes now in Houghton Library.

Each lecture introduces a major idea. James's first talk, on "Dreams and Hypnotism," focuses on the hypnagogic state, or the twilight region between waking and sleeping common to natural sleep and hypnotism. Hypnotism then becomes a means for experimentally inducing at will an otherwise inaccessible experience. His second lecture, on "Automatism," introduces the reality of subliminal consciousness—that each of us has within himself two simultaneously operating systems of intelligent consciousness, one above the threshold of awareness and one below, with its own separate characteristics. The third lecture, on "Hysteria," demonstrates the power of the buried idea. Split off from consciousness because of traumatic shock, the buried idea operates parasitically in the subconscious according to laws of its own. The fourth lecture, on "Multiple Personality," argues for the existence of a growth-oriented dimension within each personality. Although psychic fragments can often develop into seemingly independent personalities, what may emerge are permanently superior dimensions not normally accessible to waking awareness.

In the fifth lecture, on "Demoniacal Possession," James demonstrates the phenomenon of hysterical mass contagion within large populations—imitative neuropathic hysteria on a grand scale, he called it. The sixth, on "Witchcraft," clearly shows that the accusers and the judges were really insane, while many of the victims of the Inquisition and the Salem epidemic were obvious hysterics. The seventh lecture, on "Degeneration," hints at the great potential inherent in our understanding of psychosis if we would but apply the methods of the new experimental psychology of the subconscious. And in the final lecture, James shows that true geniuses are not morbid types but are, rather, the solitary heroes of humanity.

Thus, in the broad view, it appears that James establishes in the first four lectures his own understanding of a dynamic psychology of the subconscious. His second four lectures then summarize the current history of psychiatry, beginning with so-called "primitive cultures," proceeding through the Middle Ages to the modern theories of Degeneration. These final four talks show the same dynamic psychology of the subconscious that was previously developed in the first four lectures, but the subconscious, especially its pathological manifestation, is now seen at work in the social sphere.

REASONS FOR NEGLECT

We may now ask, why were these lectures overlooked? At least three factors operated to keep them in obscurity: James's own treatment of them; the later understanding by his first biographer, Ralph Barton Perry, of what they conveyed; and the subsequent reaction of other historians and biographers of various disciplines, not only to the precedents set down by Perry but also to developments in psychology and psychiatry since 1896.

First, it is obvious that James had at one time intended to publish the lectures. We can infer this from the degree of detail of his annotated notes, from the existence of at least one section of the lectures written out from the notes in readable prose, and from his family's deliberate preservation as a group of the books he used for the lectures. The books and the notes became separated only after they came to Harvard.

A likely explanation for his failure to write the talks up was the arrival of an invitation to deliver the Gifford Lectures in 1897, which shifted James's attention to a fuller concentration on religious themes and to the collection of appropriate materials. He was also concerned with philosophic rather than clinical problems at this time. In addition, his negotiations with George Howison to repeat the Exceptional Mental States Lectures at Berkeley in late 1897 fell through for financial reasons. When James finally lectured at Berkeley, he gave "Talks to Teachers" instead, and delivered the now famous address on "Philosophical Conceptions and Practical Results" in which he first introduced Peirce's pragmatism.

Also, by 1898, James had sustained injuries to his heart in a wilderness accident from which he was never to recover, making the Gifford Lectures an on-again-off-again affair. They were postponed, canceled, then reinstated at a later date as he struggled to recover sufficiently to continue his work. His 1896 lectures were not forgotten, however, for their contents contributed to major sections of several chapters in the *Varieties of Religious Experience,* particularly the chapters on Conversion, Healthy-mindedness, the Divided Self and Its Process of Unification, and his Conclusions. The notes James left undeveloped, except when he occasionally repeated one of the lectures.

Second, the treatment given to the notes by R. B. Perry led to much later confusion. To begin with, Perry listed the order of the lectures as he no doubt found them printed on the Lowell Institute announcements, without ascertaining the final order. Nor did he date their delivery correctly. Almost all subsequent references to the lectures in the history of James scholarship derive from Perry, and are usually no more than a gloss on Perry's interpretation. But James's notes give a clue to the correct order, verified through correspondence and newspaper accounts. Perry, however, apparently assumed that one of the lectures was missing and the rest out of order, for at the top of the first page of Lecture I on "Dreams and Hypnotism" he wrote:

Apparently a draft of Lecture III "Hysteria"—of Lowell Lectures of 1897—Anaesthesia due to hysteria & hypnosis—Amnesia and Dissociation—all very general and taken to prove the "wildness" of the world, similar to "What Psychical Research Has Accomplished" in *Will to Believe*.[8]

Professor Perry, eminent scholar that he was, was not able to discern James's intent, owing in no small part to the apparent loss of the lecture notes on "Automatism"; to the confusion of James's page numbering, for the numbers were continuous even though a lecture appeared to be missing; to the presence of handwritten narrative parts of Lectures I and III combined; and to the existence of several sets of extra lecture notes on similar topics, one on trance, another on degeneration, and another combining the lectures on genius and insanity.

But Perry's error may also have arisen from his implicit commitment to classical Western philosophy. He acknowledged James's interest in mysticism, the occult, and mental healing, yet he could never fathom why James held those interests in the first place. Humanistic, ethical, but ultimately Aristotelian and reasonable, Perry's biases as an intellectual scholar had already committed him to a life's work fundamentally divergent from James's—a commitment that subtly influenced him to emphasize sides of James other than those revealed by the lectures on Exceptional Mental States. He may also have concluded that since James had not developed the lectures, they were not worth dealing with.

Moreover, American philosophy after James, captured by neo-realism, positivism in science, and symbolic logic, had moved away from James's more personal and experimental point of view. Similarly, psychology, James's other chosen vocation, attempted more steadfastly to follow the lead of the natural sciences, precluding recognition of James's important contribution to altered mental states. Inner phenom-

ena became increasingly suspect, or at least they were considered irrelevant to the observable and measurable interests
of the new experimental psychology, patterned as it was after
the German laboratory tradition rather than the clinically
oriented French schools of the subconscious. For these and
other reasons, James's lecture notes have lain mostly un-
acknowledged from the time they were given to the present.

HISTORIC IMPLICATIONS

Why the lectures may be important is a more complex
question. It has been asserted, for instance, by such luminaries
as Gardner Murphy and Gordon Allport, both strong sup-
porters of James's psychology, that James had no psychology
of the subconscious, that his concept of the subliminal was
not dynamic, and that he did not say very much in the sphere
of abnormal and social psychology. These shortcomings are
sufficiently dispelled by the major themes of the Exceptional
Mental States Lectures, particularly James's emphasis on a
"dynamogenic" psychology of the subconscious and its
pathological working in the social sphere. He used this
term, "dynamogenic," in the *Varieties* and in his famous
address in 1906 on "The Energies of Men," to mean the
movement of psychic energy—in pathology when energy is
locked up and expresses itself through symptoms of depression, hallucinations, or explosive emotion; and in health
when we go beyond our normal limits and tap those vital
reserves of energy and power that each of us always holds in
abeyance. The question, he said, is how to get at these inner
reservoirs. By dynamogenic James did not mean fixed de-
velopmental stages, but rather, the evolutionary transformation of consciousness.

Evolution meant for James not simply a biological progression from past to present to future but also the realization

of potential in the immediate moment. Consciousness was a moving force in the evolutionary process. This kind of social evolution had concerned him as early as 1880 in his arguments against Social Darwinism in "Great Men, Great Thoughts, and the Environment." He considered the social self and abnormal mental states in both the *Principles* and the 1896 Lowell Lectures. Social evolution was an implicit theme in the *Varieties* when he examined extremes of religious biography and concluded that the truths of mystical experience could be tested only by their practical effects on daily life, meaning in human relationships. Certainly the themes of personal discipline, moral responsibility, and social ethics dominated his *Pragmatism* and later work on radical empiricism. Thus, the Exceptional Mental States Lectures provide a missing piece in the larger picture of James's ideas regarding character development through exploration of the subconscious. Such exploration, he thought, was a powerful tool already in the hands of each individual for constructive social change.

Another implication of the lectures is revealed by the fact that psychologists traditionally do not read what James wrote after the *Principles* in 1890, while religious scholars tend not to read him before the *Varieties* in 1902. First and foremost, his talks on Exceptional Mental States fill the gap between these two important works. Although James introduced the subliminal and multiple personality in the *Principles,* his orientation toward consciousness was then more cognitive and positivistic. By the time he published the *Varieties,* he had all but abandoned emphasis on the supremacy of reason and was busy exploring its intuitive foundations in the primacy of the mystical experience, which in turn was later absorbed into his doctrine of radical empiricism.

Not coincidentally, James's earlier formulations of the fringe or halo of consciousness developed in the Exceptional Mental States Lectures into his summary of the subliminal as defined by F. W. H. Myers, which he then incorporated into the *Varieties* as his well-known statement on the subconscious as a doorway to religious awakening. The 1896 lectures thus present a very interesting historical and conceptual link between psychology and religion.

It is also evident that the 1896 lectures attempt to summarize several significant lines of thought during a major period of James's interest in psychotherapy and psychic phenomena. That the two should somehow be related through mental healing, or that they could combine into a legitimate professional enterprise, is not outside the present bounds of the helping professions. Even in his own time James thought of the mental healing movement as something uniquely American, and as a true religious power that had to be reckoned with. But the fact that much of his work in psychology—as well as the broader scientific discipline he espoused—has been bypassed, possibly because he supported such a claim, is indirectly a measure of its strength and vitality. Indeed, as some present-day historians acknowledge, James's clear thinking on these matters stimulated the early historians of science and the academic adherents of the German laboratory tradition to define their own ground more rigorously.

Finally, James's emphasis on a psychology of the subconscious unique to each individual is most intriguing, for it implies a psychotherapeutic method allied as much with philosophy and religion as with experimental medicine and psychology: one based ultimately on understanding of the patient's problem followed by self-help, rather than on professional diagnosis by classification followed by impersonal treatment. The one orientation stresses independence through education, while the other stresses dependent care.

That the helping professions have grown away from this ideal is attested to by the oblivion that has been the fate of many of James's students, colleagues, and friends who espoused such an orientation, many of whom became pioneers in their chosen fields: George Miller Beard, pioneer in the sexual exhaustion theory of the neurosis in the 1880s; Silas Weir Mitchell, poet-neurologist, famous for his diet and rest cures; Bernard Sachs, founder of neurology at Mount Sinai Hospital in New York; Boris Sidis, who recognized the healing significance of the hypnoid state; Morton Prince, famous for his studies of multiple personality; Elwood Worcester, Leipzig Ph.D. in philosophy and Episcopal priest, who linked psychotherapy and religion in Boston's Emmanuel movement; Louville Eugene Emerson, who earned his Ph.D. under James and became the first clinical psychologist to practice at Massachusetts General Hospital, from 1911 until his death in 1939; C. G. Jung, completely ignored in the psychiatric curriculum of our medical schools, whose formulations on the collective unconscious and psychological types were significantly influenced by James; William McDougall, James's friend, successor to Münsterberg's chair in psychology at Harvard, and later founder of the famous parapsychology clinic at Duke University—all are distinguished examples.[9]

These men were some of the first to recognize and support Sigmund Freud, although many later became Freud's harshest critics. As Morton Prince once remarked, "Freudian psychology had flooded the field like a full rising tide and the rest of us were left submerged like clams buried in the sands at low water."[10] But what if such an alternative view had captivated the interest of the helping professions? What if clinical and academic psychology had merged at such a point? And is not such a view just as viable today as in James's time, or perhaps even more so because of the current crisis in psychiatry, with its overreliance on drugs and shock therapy and the once functional but now limited acceptance of psychoanalytic definitions of the unconscious? Could not a more encompassing definition of inner experience or a broader view of the whole person be embodied in James's contribution to psychopathology? As James himself would probably say, though history may inform us of this possibility, only our own practical experience can demonstrate the results.

: LECTURE I :

DREAMS AND HYPNOTISM

William James begins his first Lowell Lecture with the idea that the main difficulty we have in understanding abnormal mental states undoubtedly lies more in our attitudes toward them than in the absolutely fixed character of the phenomena themselves.[1] "The less we think of the morbid," his notes say, the better. "Think of it *morbidly*," that is, a state in flux and always related to other, healthier conditions simultaneously present in mental life. "We make a common distinction between healthy and morbid," he tells his audience, "but the true fact is that we cannot make it sharp. No one symptom by itself is a morbid one—it depends rather on the part that it plays. We speak of melancholy and moral tendencies, but he would be a bold man who should say that melancholy was not an essential part of every character. Saint Paul, Lombroso, Kant,[2] each is in some way an example of how melancholy in a life gives a truer sense of values." Thus James establishes the major theme of the series: "A life healthy on the whole must have some morbid elements."

"Sleep," for example, "would be a dreadful disease but for its familiarity." Likewise, "we do not regard dreaming as morbid because it is customary, but if it were not, it would

be the subject of much medical wonder." Yet sleep may become pathological, just as dreaming may interfere with consciousness in already abnormal conditions. "It can be really
dreadful for hysterics," James says, citing a case presented by
Richard von Krafft-Ebing, pioneer in forensic psychiatry and
founder of modern scientific investigations on sexual psychopathology.[3] James's notes give no specific reference to
Krafft-Ebing's work, but he may have been thinking of a
well-known case in which Krafft-Ebing mentioned the influence of dreams on the development of symptoms in a
Hungarian woman of twenty-nine, named Ilma Schander.[4]

"If dreams don't interfere with waking life," James continues, "they only enlarge our knowledge" of it. The same
applies with "various intoxicants."[5] While we are in these
partial states, they appear to be all there is to reality, as if no
other state exists but the one we are momentarily experiencing. Even our experience of everyday waking reality may
be only a "fragment" of the whole. "Who shall say that the
ordinary experience is the only one possible?"[6] In other
words, we seem too familiar with the waking state and at the
same time show little knowledge or understanding of these
other conditions.

"Now dreaming is a primary characteristic of some states
[of consciousness]," the lecture notes continue, "so it be-
hooves us to ask about the difference between the waking and
the dreaming mind." James then launches into an exposition
of mental operations in waking and dreaming, emphasizing
the normal dream experience. In dreaming, all "associations
are complete." The "whole of knowledge is brought to bear."
We are all familiar with this experience when we dream, as
any image before the mind can have many associations with
other ideas or images both directly and indirectly related to
the dream content. This is not usually so in the waking
state, where ideas are allowed expression only by controlled
associations that give logical continuity to the progression of
our thoughts. Waking reality, by its very nature, has a ten-

dency to exclude apparently random associations, while at the same time it admits only those ideas most pertinent to the object of attention.[7]

James then says that if someone were to yell "House on fire," in a large gathering, three types of responses would reveal the differing conditions of association: the "level-headed," the "rattled," and the "half-awake." The first type exhibits a rationally cool and calm state of consciousness, quite present and alert, which associates the call with danger, danger with the probable source, and knowledge of the source with all the most viable means of escape. The second, or rattled, type is aware of the call of danger and recognizes it, but may lack the kind of spontaneous alertness that would suggest alternative strategies for mobilization. The half-awake, only partly present, type is liable at any time to interpret events in a semi-dream consciousness, is readily able to imagine things that never happened, and is unable to remember later the difference between dreaming and waking reality.

In dreams, James continues, "ideas are detached from their usual consorts," that is, ideas normally associated with objects or events in the external world appear in the dream, but are now dissociated from their material referents. The lecture then cites an example from one of James's own dreams, "my dream of Seth"—perhaps referring to Andrew Seth Pringle-Pattison, one of James's friends and philosophical correspondents.[8]

There are two primary characteristics of the dream, James explains: a "narrowing" of the field of consciousness, which is a "negative" quality; and a "vividness" of the contents that remain, which is "positive." In other words, when the field of consciousness narrows, attention becomes more and more restricted, forcing all other ideas out of the picture. What objects remain before the mind's eye become more intense, vivid, and lively, as if they were borrowing energy from the other mental objects that are excluded.

Narrowing occurs only in certain states, while vividness occurs in almost all; but both are experienced in dreaming. James then makes the point that these two characteristics are "found in many disorders" soon to be described.[9]

"So get a clear idea of [this one] fundamental fact!" he stresses. "The sound mind is a system of ideas in gear, integrated [with every other idea, and having] a field, a focus, and a margin; the margin [however] *controls.*" In other words, the widest possible association of meanings in the interpretation of an idea is what constitutes the sound mind.[10] "In a healthy life, there are no single ideas! The abstract law is that each idea by itself tends to be believed and acted out. This does not usually happen in waking reality, and yet, *this is exactly what happens in dreams.*"[11] In other words, while single ideas do not stand alone in waking life, they may do so in the dream state.[12]

James then follows with an "electric wire and chandelier metaphor," but the lecture notes give no other details. Apparently he is still contrasting the processes of association of ideas in the waking and dreaming states. A similar chandelier metaphor was used by George Miller Beard, the New York neurologist and specialist on trance consciousness, who was a pioneer in electrotherapeutics, in a monograph on trance consciousness with which James was undoubtedly familiar. Beard used his chandelier metaphor to describe the difference between ordinary sleep, trance, and death. When all the burners of a chandelier are fully lighted, that is the normal waking state; when all the burners are turned down low, but not turned out entirely—as in a public hall before the start of entertainment—that is ordinary sleep; if we turn out all the burners entirely except one, and that one, as often happens, flames all the more brightly from the increased pressure, that is trance; and if all the burners are turned out entirely, that is death. Trance, Beard said, is a concentration of nervous activity in some one direction, with corresponding suspension of nervous activity in other directions.[13]

The overemphasis of a single idea to the exclusion of all others, followed by further elaboration and related associations, is an unusual state of mental affairs. But there are analogies "in waking life which approach this condition," says James. He names four: "the day-dreaming of a milk maid"; spinning "castles in the air," for example, the "absorption [of] Newton"; the "drunkenness" caused by alcohol; and "sleep-drunkenness," produced when the sleeper is active but only half awake.

No annotated references illumine his first two examples, but all of us can recall experiencing those waking fantasies that occur during moments of distraction, or the flood of ideas that may come from focusing intensely on one idea for extended periods, as in moments of creative imagination. In mentioning Newton, James is suggesting that the key to Newton's mind was his unusual power of continuous concentrated introspection, his ability to hold a problem in his mind for hours, days, even weeks until it surrendered its secret.[14]

In his third example, James cites an episode from Emile Erckmann and Alexandre Chatrian's novel *L'Ami Fritz* (1867) as a modern instance of happy unconsciousness under the influence of alcohol. While traveling in Germany as a medical student, James had first read the book the year it was published, and it became for him one of those "golden books" that "renewed one's belief in the succulent harmonies of creation," because it was founded on a wholesome and reassuring humanity.

James recounts a drinking episode that involved the hero Fritz, Suzel, his sweetheart, her father, and other friends. The group has assembled in the large empty dining room of an inn. As Suzel and her father drive up in a carriage, Fritz points a champagne bottle out of the window and pops the cork off in their direction. At the same time he yells a toast. Suzel imagines the sound of the traditional wedding gun; her father imagines Fritz merely drunk.

Once inside, the guests proceed to empty the bottles of champagne. Suddenly someone asks of the whole group: "And how do you like the wine?" One person replies that it reminds him of French culture; another argues in favor of the German life. No one seems to pay attention to the political debate that develops. Instead, Suzel's father gazes out the window, thinking of his coming harvest. He mutters to himself, "The wine is good, the wine is good," while some of the others strike up a conversation about the relation of the wine to the good weather they have been having. Meanwhile, Fritz and Suzel are gazing intently into each other's eyes, enraptured by their mutual attention. They can only say, "How good it is," meaning their feelings for each other at the moment, rather than the wine they are drinking. Another friend looks at them but is aware of nothing because he is so absorbed in his own reverie.[15]

From this James concludes that alcohol does induce a form of trance consciousness that, as in dreaming, can more easily overemphasize a single idea at the expense of all others.[16]

The fourth example James gives of waking experiences that approximate the dream state is taken from Wilhelm Wundt, pioneer in the German experimental laboratory tradition that was imported to American universities in the 1880s. James retells Wundt's account of an event, later published in *Philosophische Studien,* that took place in the winter of 1885 when Wundt was a medical assistant living in the Department for Women at Heidelberg Hospital. For several days he had been awakened each night to consult with very sick patients and was exhausted by insufficient sleep after his strenuous day's work. When awakened, Wundt would dress himself in a half-drowsy, sleep-drunken state, visit patients, and order whatever was necessary, without total awareness. Whatever needed to be done, he did mechanically.

One night he was awakened to see a typhus patient who in her delirium was disturbing her roommates. Wundt acted as if fully awake, though in reality he was in a dream state not unlike her own. While he appeared to talk normally with the nurses and gave appropriate responses, he later remembered not being wholly conscious. A sedative was indicated for the patient, and Wundt's eyes lighted on a glass bottle sitting on the dispensary shelf that contained tincture of iodine; he erroneously told himself that this was the appropriate medication. He asked the nurse for the bottle and a spoon, and the two of them sat the patient up. Wundt tried to give the medicine, but the patient pushed the spoon out of her mouth, spat the contents on the floor, and refused the rest.

Wundt was greatly surprised, for though he knew it to be iodine, he had unconsciously superimposed onto this brown liquid the properties of laudanum, a liquid sedative of the same color stored by the clinic in the same kind of bottle. His behavior suggested some confusion, to the nurse's discomfort. On the way back to his room everything became clear to him, and he realized that he had acted while in a somnambulistic state. Concerned for the safety of the patient, he went next morning to confer with his professor, who assured him that no harm was done.[17]

So daydreaming, abstract thinking under conditions of intense concentration, alcoholic intoxication, and "sleep-drunkenness" are all experiences in normal waking life that are similar to our mental processes while dreaming. Each person responds to such episodes in a different way. "Now some minds get easily out of gear and go to pieces," James continues, while "others have a broad field and keep together. Why this is so, why minds differ, is one of the great questions in theoretic psychology. As yet, there is very little contribution to its solution."[18]

One explanation that James offers came from Pierre Janet, the distinguished French philosopher, physician, and pioneer in the psychopathology of the subconscious.[19] James was to draw heavily from Janet for the 1896 Exceptional Mental States Lectures, particularly from Janet's ideas on dissociation and the synthesizing capacity of consciousness. In a series of articles that began in 1886 and culminated in his *L'Automatisme psychologique* in 1889, Janet had postulated that various phenomena of altered mental states follow from an incapacity to fix the attention, due to mental or moral weakness. Such weakness, he believed, may be due to hereditary depletion of the nerve force, but shows itself only after a series of traumatic or exhausting experiences, which then exert a negative effect on the synthesizing functions of the brain. When the capacity for sustained and directed attention is dispersed, dissociation of certain parts of consciousness from waking life occurs, thus casting psychic fragments into the subconscious. This weakening allows elements of a normally subconscious secondary existence to displace waking awareness, at which time we become more susceptible to suggestion and to hypnosis.

Janet called this altered state "somnambulism," a term in vogue in French psychology at the time. By somnambulism he meant a second psychological existence, clearly distinct from the first and alternating with it, a state in which the intellectual phenomena are sufficiently developed for the subject to perceive the sensations and even to understand the signs and language of normal experience, but a state that is nevertheless totally forgotten when the subject returns to the normal condition.[20] The French investigators also called this *"dédoublement de la conscience,"* referring to symptoms that arise from the doubling of consciousness, in which a normally subwaking existence takes control and two separate states occur simultaneously in the same field of awareness.

James then presents examples of "natural somnambulism," referring to extremes of everyday experience that can produce such alterations in consciousness. He cites the work of T. D.

Crothers, superintendent of a sanitarium for inebriates in Connecticut, who was a specialist in alcohol intoxication, and George Miller Beard, who had popularized the term "neurasthenia," meaning nerve weakness. Crothers had written a monograph on *The Trance State in Inebriety* (1882), about workers whose jobs were exhausting and monotonous, to which Beard contributed an introduction.[21]

James's lecture notes cite several examples from this work. In one case, a steamboat captain had informed Crothers that if he drank a glass or more of brandy when he was worn out by lack of sleep, all memory of time and place would vanish. Some hours later he would recover and find that, though he had remained at his post, he was unable to remember what had happened during the blank period. To his associates the captain had seemed no different from his usual self, only less talkative.

In another case, Crothers described a skilled mechanic who reported similar blank intervals while operating a dangerous machine after drinking alcohol. Though he could perform all his duties, which required skill and judgment, he could not remember anything that had taken place during a period of several hours. He would awaken when the machine stopped for the night. When the machine was kept in motion later than usual one night, his blank state continued until it stopped.

Crothers also wrote of a house painter, an inebriate, who could paint for hours in the most dangerous positions while in this kind of trance state, but after coming down and recovering his senses would wonder how he could have done so without falling.

In the same monograph, Beard reported that while traveling in Switzerland, he had encountered another remarkable illustration of the natural induction of such a state. There was a tremendous landslide in which part of a mountain fell on a village, killing a number of people. Some of those who were near and in peril but managed to escape were frightened into a state resembling drunkenness, in which they walked about in a kind of natural somnambulism. They were never able to give a trustworthy account of what had happened. The emotion of fear had produced the same effect as the emotion of expectation in inducing these states, which, in turn, had the same effect that alcohol or bromide might produce. It was known that there had been at least two separate landslides, but whether they were separated by a minute or an hour was never determined, since the traumatic memories of the inhabitants who survived were destroyed or impaired by fear.[22] "In [all] these [naturally occurring] states" described by Janet, Crothers, and Beard, say James's notes, "memory is [completely] gone."

"Now hypnotism," his notes continue, thus introducing one of the most important experimental methods then known for artificially inducing subliminal states of consciousness. Hypnotism, it was thought, allowed controlled observation of states strikingly similar to natural somnambulism, in that it also appeared to break up the mind into two or more parts.[23]

The prevailing theory of the time was that in the normal condition of the mind, the waking state and the subliminal consciousness work in perfect harmony, blended into a unity that we know as one conscious personality. Waking consciousness is normally at the forefront, while the subliminal remains obscured but at work in the background. In hypnosis, the two systems are dissociated. Waking consciousness is split off from the rest of the nervous system, while subliminal consciousness is laid bare and comes into direct contact with the external world. Characteristics of normally subdued states of consciousness can then be observed; and in this condition the hypnotized subject will more easily receive instructions and perform actions suggested by the hypnotist.

"You know its history," James notes. "Discovered by [Franz Anton] Mesmer and rediscovered since, hypnosis first met with denial of the facts by scientists, until suddenly orthodox opinion admitted them. It was the theory of suggestion, however, that finally robbed hypnotism of its former marvel. Mesmer's theory of a fluid through all of nature, later theories that it was the will of the strong over the weak —all these explanations are now exploded.[24]

"Hypnotism, in fact, may be only partial sleep, for if the hypnotizer leaves, the patient either wakes up entirely or falls into a deep, natural sleep and may begin to snore."[25] Moreover, the hypnotizer "needn't have a strong will at all; you need only suggest an idea which the mind itself takes hold of. But the subject's mind can only be hypnotized in its passage from the waking to the sleeping state. All persons go through this hypnotic [hypnagogic] state twice a day. A good subject is one who can be caught on the road to sleep and suspended—that is, prevented from deep sleep. If the mind of the subject is caught at just this point and given a suggestion, it immediately acts upon that idea. Everything depends on the subject allowing himself to be entranced, and hardly anything on the operator, except that he must engender the subject's trust and be able to fix attention on the relaxed condition."[26]

"The main symptom is *suggestibility*," notes James. By this he means the intrusion into the mind of an idea that is at first met with opposition by the person, then accepted uncritically, and realized unreflectively, almost automatically. In turn, "this means vividness and motor efficacy." Vividness occurs when one idea produces an intense emotional excitement that banishes all other ideas and creates a state of monoideism, or concentration of consciousness on that single idea.[27] By motor efficacy, James is alluding to the ease with which the idea can then be translated into muscular activity. Suggestibility refers to an increase in the reflex ideo-motor, ideo-sensitive, and ideo-sensorial excitability. "This is unquestionably the true explanation," concludes James.*

"Some persons are suggestible when awake," he then points out. By acting on the emotion of expectation in a sensitive subject, by saying of some task, "you can't do it," not only is the doing paralyzed, "but [whatever] opposite muscles [there may be that are necessary to the action are liable to] contract."

Several examples follow: an instance of heightened suggestibility that involved his daughter Peggy, "on her bicycle"; and a case quoted from the New York neurologist William Alexander Hammond, in which someone apparently "breaks a table." Some notes then follow that may refer to particular hypnotized subjects, but details are lacking.[28]

Other examples of suggestibility might include the sensation we experience at the thought of being tickled, the yawn that follows someone else's, the feat of strength we think beyond us until we work ourselves up and perform the act; and of course the excessive suggestibility seen in crowds excited by religious, political, or other forms of enthusiasm.

In all these instances we find a stream of consciousness

---

* In his review of Hans Schmidkunz's *Psychologie der Suggestion*, James concurred that "we must regard the hypnotic trance as a genuinely peculiar state, carrying increased suggestibility in its train." This was contrary to the prevailing view, espoused by Hippolyte Bernheim, the French physician who founded a school of suggestive therapeutics at Nancy. Bernheim felt that there was no such thing as a hypnoid state; rather, hypnosis was due to suggestibility alone. James's view, however, is that with the fall of the threshold of consciousness a single idea could be implanted which would appear isolated and personified—that is, blown out of proportion. Such a single idea could then easily lead to motor activity, but only when this opening of the doors to the subliminal had taken place. See W. James, Review of Schmidkunz's *Psychologie der Suggestion* in the *Philosophical Review*, 1 (1892), 306–309; and James's copy of Schmidkunz's *Der Hypnotismus in gemeinfasslicher Darstellung* (Stuttgart: A. Zinner, n.d.), Houghton Library, Harvard.

that is flowing along in its individual, idiosyncratic way; suddenly it is interrupted from the depths by a wave that rises to the surface, swamps the other waves, overflows the banks, deflects for a while the course of the current, and then as suddenly subsides, so that the stream resumes its natural course, flowing once more in its former bed. On tracing the cause of this disturbance, we invariably find that it is due to some external source, to some other stream running alongside the one disturbed.[29] In all such cases, the "suggestibility" —as James's notes state, echoing Janet's theories—"is due to the narrowness of the field of consciousness."

We see a similar condition of this narrowness in dreaming, according to James. "Dreaming [is a] disease of sleep" in which visual imagery may be produced by both internal or external means. It may result internally from random activity of the nervous system, or it may result externally from sources in the environment; in either case, there is a narrowing of attention as the subject enters the hypnagogic state.[30] Drawing an analogy between hallucinations suggested under hypnosis and those suggested while in natural sleep, James goes on to suggest that in both hypnosis and sleep, "the senses are dead; but *if*" dreaming could be induced from external sources in natural sleep as well as in the artificial sleep of hypnosis, further evidence would be provided that sleep and hypnosis are analogous. In one state we call the phenomenon dreaming, in the other we call it hallucination; but the underlying hypnagogic stratum is the same.[31]

James then reviews the work of Alfred Maury, a famous French archeologist who had interpreted thousands of his own dreams and had coined the term *"illusions hypnago-giques"* to refer to phenomena witnessed in this impressionable state between waking and sleeping. Maury would have his assistant provoke him with various sorts of stimulation just after he had fallen asleep. Perfume under Maury's nose made him dream he was in a perfume shop in Cairo; a match under his feet made him dream of walking across coals; and so on.[32]

James tells his audience of one instance in which Maury was tickled with a feather, resulting in a dream that he was being tortured by having the skin of his face torn off by a mask of hot pitch[33] In a second example, James's notes cite "head on anvil: water." This concerned the auditory origin of some dreams. Maury recounted that the heat of the day had made him drowsy. He fell asleep and dreamed that his head had been placed on an anvil and was being hammered on in double time. He heard very clearly in his dream the noise of the heavy hammers, but for some reason, instead of his head shattering, it melted into water. He woke up, felt his face covered with perspiration, and from the courtyard next door heard the very real noise of hammering.[34]

A separate set of lecture notes found among James's papers, entitled "Sleep-Trance," contains more information on the induction of dream images from external sources that occur during natural sleep. Along with an English translation of examples from Maury's *Le Sommeil et les rêves,* there is an article on "Dream Excitation" by James Mark Baldwin, cut from an 1888 issue of *Science.* According to Baldwin, although Maury demonstrated the direct influence of slight sense stimuli on the flow of our dream consciousness, this phenomenon is difficult to confirm under ordinary circumstances. Baldwin reported a case that occurred naturally to him: "On the night of October 22, I had a dream which perfectly fulfills the conditions of Maury's experiments. I fell asleep about eleven o'clock, and found myself with a companion in a wood watching a number of woodcutters at work. After I looked at them for some time, one of the workmen drew my attention quite suddenly by giving forth a strange sound, half musical and half speech, by which he seemed to be trying to express something to his neighbor; and the sound came with every blow of his axe in regular rhythm. The sound seemed to me distinctly familiar and yet very strange, and I turned to my friend and said, 'What an apology for conversation!' Just as I spoke, I awoke, and the sound of the peculiar tone of the clock downstairs striking twelve broke in upon my consciousness. The four remaining strokes of the clock preserved exactly the rhythm of the wood-chopper's axe; and not only so, but the sense of familiarity which had puzzled me in the dream was relieved with a glow of pleasure as I recognized the sound of the clock."[35]

James provides these examples to illustrate that hypnagogic imagery could be induced from external sources during natural sleep. Next he turns to examples of hypnagogic imagery induced under hypnosis. His notes show that he drew here on the work of Philippe Tissié, a French physician interested in fatigue, fugue states (that is, passing in and out of a state with complete loss of memory of it afterward), and various forms of exercise and training related to sports. Tissié had published a volume of his studies on dream imagery in hospital patients prone to somnambulism. Since these patients were easily hypnotizable, they made good subjects for Tissié's studies in dream suggestion. James's notes mention "lantern of nurse," which refers to an idea which one patient had carried over into the dream state from the waking condition, and his subsequent confusion of these two states. The patient, Philippe Troit, wanted some wine. He dreamed that one evening he left the hospital and went to his boss to get two bottles of wine. The boss gave them to Troit, who took a third one on credit. Returning to the hospital by the same route, Troit put the wine on a shelf above the headboard of his bed. He then went to bed and, rubbing his hands, said to himself, "Mr. Boisvert [the superintendent] doesn't want to let me go out—well, I've played a trick on him."

The next morning he saw the nurse with two or three patients who, by the dim light of a lantern, were drinking his wine and making fun of him. A moment later he woke up and told the nurse as she was passing by that he had seen four people drinking his wine right in front of him. "My dream was so vivid," he added, "that as I left, I went to see

my boss to ask him if he'd given me two bottles of wine.
When I heard his negative, I was very surprised."[36]
James then gives the audience another example of dream
induction, this time concerning a subject in a state of
hypnosis. His notes read: "tickle forehead—bees," and it is
reasonable to assume that he was referring from memory to
an episode cited in Tissié's *Les Rêves*. This involved a
somnambulistic patient called Albert, who had been hypnotized and then, while his eyes were closed, had his forehead
tickled with a feather, which produced the sensation of in-
sects flying around him (actually the subject spoke of flies,
not bees). Tissié reported that Albert said: "These flies are
unbearable; how can you work with such wind and so many
flies!" "Can you see the flies?" Tissié asked him. "No," Albert
said, "but I feel them." He tried to swat them with his hand.
"It's funny how they came so suddenly." However, he
tolerated the tickling very easily.[37]
Tissié then blew a short puff of air into the hypnotized
subject's face as he continued to stroke his forehead with the
feather. "What wind!" Albert said. "All these flies, all
these lice! My whole body has been stung! I feel ants!" He
began to scratch and slap his legs.[38]
James's purpose in giving these examples is to suggest the
appropriate conditions needed if external stimulation is to
have an effect on dream imagery. When the subject was in a
highly suggestible state, he could be easily influenced; "hence
hallucinations," which are accompanied by the usual
"dramatic scenes."
"Yet why doesn't he wake from this stimulation? He will
if the suggestions produce a sufficient disturbance," James
infers. "Otherwise, as in regular dreams, a synthesis [of the
external stimulus with the internal dream imagery] will
occur. . . . So long as he *doesn't* wake, then the analogy between the artificial and the natural state of dreaming is
complete."
James concludes this first lecture with a summary com-

paring natural and hypnotically induced sleep, in which he focuses on six phenomena common to both.

1. "Both wake when you say wake." In natural sleep, it is possible to implant the suggestion of waking at a given time, the most common example of which is to tell yourself on retiring that you wish to arise at a certain time the next morning, and lo! you awaken at precisely that hour, even to that minute. In hypnotically induced sleep, awakening may be simply a matter of getting the subject's prior consent that he will awaken automatically from the trance at a prearranged signal.

2. "Both are anaesthetic to most impressions." As soon as the senses become dormant during sleep, we are oblivious to external impressions. We remain unmoved by the onslaught of noises in the street, conversations, the hum of machinery; in short, we are impervious to anything that is ordinary and within our expectations. Similarly, in hypnotically induced sleep, sensory stimulation is reduced to a minimum, perhaps to nothing but the hypnotizer's voice, and even that can be suggested out of the hypnotized person's awareness.

3. "In both, there is a possible *rapport*." As we have seen, it is possible for a person in the waking state to influence the images of a sleeping person under certain experimental situations.* A mother in ordinary sleep will awaken at any

---

* In his assessment of *Telepathic Dreams, Experimentally Induced,* by Dr. G. B. Ermancora of Padua (*Psychological Review*, 3 [1896], 99–100), James gives an account of the telepathic induction of dreams induced in two simultaneously sleeping subjects, a medium and her spirit control, "Elvira." The younger sister often dreamed of the medium's spirit-control, so Ermancora hypnotized the medium and instructed "Elvira" to dream certain dreams, which were then picked up at night and dreamed by the medium's younger sister. Experimental precautions were taken to avoid any communication of the content of each dream to the younger sister beforehand. James himself told of being present at one of these successful experiments, although he doubted that rational, scientific men would ever believe the results.

slight noise made by her infant, while she will sleep
through much louder disturbances that have another cause.
Likewise, it is the personality of the hypnotist that trans-
fers from the waking state to the hypnotically induced
one.[39]

4. "Suggestions are obeyed in both." James's notes here
cite "Delboeuf" and "Hodson" on the aftereffects of suggestion produced under hypnosis. There is also a note on
"Mrs. Morris's cases."

Joseph Delboeuf—a Belgian scientist and philosopher, and
colleague of the French philosopher Charles Renouvier, as
well as critic of the neurologist Jean-Martin Charcot—had
been a friend of James's since 1882. James referred to
Delboeuf's experiments on suggestion in his chapter on
Hypnotism in the *Principles*. Delboeuf had produced two
symmetrical burns on the skin of a hypnotized patient and
then suggested that one would be painful and the other not.
The result was a dry scorch with no scar on the side with
suggested anaesthesia, whereas on the painful side a regular
blister with suppuration and subsequent scarring occurred.
The implication was that suggesting away pain early could
prevent inflammation later.[40]

"Hodson" probably refers to Richard Hodgson, a founding
member of the English Society for Psychical Research, who
moved to the United States in order to help James establish
an American branch, and to take over investigation of the
Belmont medium, Leonora Piper, whom James had first discovered in 1885. James's reference probably concerns Hodgson's report, "Evidence as to Mr. Barrow's Experiments in
Suggestion Without Hypnotism," which is cited in the *Proceedings of the English Society for Psychical Research* for
1896.[41]

The case of Mrs. Morris undoubtedly refers to the sworn
statements of Mrs. Alice Vanderbilt Morris on the effects of

sleep suggestion that enhance the performance of complex tasks when later awake.[42]

5. "Memory is often gone in both." A subject awakening from hypnosis usually has a complete amnesia for all that has happened. Similarly, when we awaken from sleep, even if we retain fragments of a dream, unless they are exceptionally vivid, we usually forget them rapidly. Often we do not remember our dreams at all; in fact, the less we remember, the more we are convinced that we have slept soundly. There are instances, however, in which memory is "sometimes preserved from one dream to the next," a phenomenon that is readily observed in successive hypnotic sessions. James's notes here refer to studies by Hippolyte Bernheim, who was Jean-Martin Charcot's chief rival in the interpretation of the mechanism of hypnosis. Bernheim had successfully demonstrated that the memory for events occurring under hypnosis could be transferred to the subject's dreams during natural sleep.[43]

6. In both sleep and hypnosis, we see the aftereffects of a suggestion that is implanted in one state appearing in another. James then compares the "post-effects" of sleep—"as noted above," his notes tell us—to the effects of post-hypnotic suggestion in the dreams of certain hysteric patients. He cites the case of "Albert's fugues" described by Tissié.

Albert, the subject of a previous example, was a patient of Tissié's who was prone to somnambulistic states during which he would lose his identity for long periods. James may have been referring to an instance in which Albert had said, "Every time I dream that I have been bitten or beaten, I suffer all day in the part attacked," implying that suggestions in dream life can have effects that carry over into waking reality, just as a suggestion under hypnosis can be acted out at a later time.[44]

"In all this," says James finally, "we notice *dissociation,* polyzoism,* or polypsychism," in other words, a plurality of states, or consciousness split into several parts. "This conception held to," he concludes, "throws a flood of light on matter to be introduced in later lectures."

* "The property, in a complex organism, of being composed of minor quasi-independent organisms"—F. W. H. Myers, *Human Personality and Its Survival of Bodily Death* (New York: Longmans, Green, 1907 edn.), p. xvi.

: LECTURE II :

AUTOMATISM

Summarizing his first lecture, James outlined the importance of the hypnagogic state—the ultra-marginal zone of consciousness through which each of us passes twice daily, once on entering and once on waking from sleep. Hypnosis, he suggested, may be a method of temporarily suspending consciousness in its transition from waking to sleeping, and so may provide us with an experimental method for the study not only of the normal condition but also of deeper sources of pathology. A comparison of dreams and hypnotic reproductions then drew James to his conclusion that "the mind seems to embrace a confederation of psychic entities."[1]

James opens his second lecture by saying that "two kinds of phenomena met with in the hypnotic trance . . . especially bring out" this splitting apart of the mind into different states: "negative hallucinations" and "post-hypnotic suggestion." Negative hallucinations are "systematized anaesthesias"—especially of the skin and the eye, suggested during hypnosis. Post-hypnotic suggestion refers to commands given in trance that are then carried out unconsciously upon awakening. We are particularly fortunate in having a fully written out version of this portion of James's notes that corresponds almost exactly with his lecture outline.[2]

"A good hypnotic subject," he writes, "may, as is well known, have all sorts of hallucinations suggested to him. He will see things and animals where they are not; marks, drawings, etc., will appear to him on a blank sheet of paper, if only you tell him they are there. Not only this but you may suggest to him *negative* hallucinations. He shall *not* see a certain mark, a certain word in a printed sentence, a certain object in the room. He shall not hear a certain person's words.

"Such phenomena are proved not sensorial by many facts," James notes, "especially those brought to light by M. Féré and Meyer regarding the production of negative after-images.[3] If a subject is made blind to a certain patch of color, it is well known that in its place the subject will see the complementary color of the one not seen. If many lines are drawn on a blackboard and the subject is instructed to be blind only to a certain one, that particular line will be seen unless it is in some way marked to distinguish its absence from the others in the group. The subject must first recognize the line before it is selected as the one to be omitted.

"Bernheim,[4] in other experiments, makes the hypnotized subject deaf, then commands her to now hear—and she hears. He makes another girl remember" her insensitivity to his touches to her nose, a roll of paper, her ear, and so on. "One eye is made blind, yet when the subject looks through a prism the image doubles" as it does normally. Similar phenomena occur with hearing. This "looks like shamming," comments James. "She has doubtless heard him with her ears all the time. But the hearing had entered into no connection with her thoughts or behavior, until the permissive suggestion was made.

"The state of mind here is very peculiar. There is no sensorial insensibility, and no mere failure to notice through ordinary inattention. It is a mental deafness and blindness which is more complex, something like an active dissociation or shutting out of certain feelings and objects from the field of consciousness that counts a thought and governs conduct. It is as when one 'cuts' an acquaintance, 'ignores a claim,' or refuses to be influenced by a consideration to which nevertheless one remains 'marginally' and ineffectively aware. I say marginally, but the difficult question to answer even in these cases, is whether the idea excluded from influence is really inside the margin of the conscious field or outside of it altogether, forming a separate but co-existent bit of flickering all alone by itself. It would seem to quiver directly *on* the limit in these simple hypnotic instances, sometimes being in and sometimes being out, and at all times ready to make connection.

"But in other cases it is surely extra-marginal altogether, and the subject's mind loses its quality of unity, and lapses into a polypsychism of fields that genuinely co-exist and yet are outside of each other's ken and dissociated functionally. From all quarters of the pathological and experimental horizon this state of facts is borne in upon us. I can only give a few examples to familiarize you, if you are not already familiar, with so strange and unexpected a phenomenon.

"It was first brought to light in a distinct way by Edmund Gurney's investigation into post-hypnotic suggestion,"[5] James continues. "In a considerable number of hypnotic subjects an order given during induced sleep to do something at a designated moment after waking, will be punctually obeyed, even although, on being waked, the subject's mind will preserve no recollection of the order, nor indeed of any of the other trance occurrences. The order may be to perform it simply after the lapse of time of a designated interval, whether days, hours, or minutes. One can suggest paralysis, sleep, dreams, cures, anaesthesias, motor acts, and also hallucinations, both auditory and visual."[6]

James then introduces several illustrative examples of experiments in post-hypnotic suggestion reported by Albert Moll of Berlin and Jules Liègeois of Nancy. Both men were followers of A. A. Liébeault, a pioneer in psychotherapy with hypnosis, and Bernheim's teacher. Moll had pioneered hypnotic therapy in Germany in the mid-1880s, later making a major contribution to the field of sexual psychopathology. Liègeois, a lawyer by profession, and one of the four major representatives of the famous Nancy school of suggestive therapeutics, was chiefly interested in the influence of suggestion on crime.

Both Moll and Liègeois had studied the effects of post-hypnotic suggestion carried out over varying lengths of time. In each case, the subject was placed in a hypnotic trance and a suggestion was given to him to be carried out at some future date, always without the subject's remembering the command once he had returned to the waking state. James tells his audience that Moll had suggested to a subject: "You will come to my house on the sixteenth Tuesday, reckoning from last Tuesday, and will abuse all the people present." This suggestion succeeded completely, although no precise date was named.[7] In a case of one of the longest periods of time between hypnotic suggestion and performance recorded, Liègeois and Liébeault suggested to a subject that "an entire year elapse before a command was acted out, which was then performed on the exact hour and day of the succeeding interval."[8] It is a great puzzle how these suggestions can be carried out so exactly, and it was to the genius of Edmund Gurney's experiments that James again turned for an explanation of the facts that suggested the operation of a simultaneous double consciousness.

James notes that Gurney had published several articles on different degrees of hypnotism and trance and their effects on post-hypnotic states, "involving a person referred to only as 'P-ll.' " Gurney's subject, P-ll, was "given a letter and told to mail it on the 123rd day" after the suggestion was implanted. During that interval the subject had "no memory [whatever of the command], but when returned to the hypnotic trance," it was found that he had been keeping an unconscious "record of the days that had passed"—so accurately, in fact, that he could give the number of hours and minutes left.[9]

Even when a "sovereign was offered" to the subject when not under hypnosis to induce him to account for the number of days that had elapsed, James notes that the subject was unable to recall the command and claimed ignorance of anything that had actually happened. If Gurney suggested to P-ll while hypnotized, "You will get up and poke the fire in six minutes," and if, after having been awakened, the subject was then put back into the hypnotic condition within that interval, it was found that he would report something like "three and a half more, poke the fire."[10] These examples, James's notes suggest, point to the operation of a secondary intelligence, attending to its own affairs and not interfering with ordinarily active consciousness.

The notes then cite the arguments against the existence of such a secondary intelligent consciousness that had been put forward by A. H. Pierce, a psychologist and one of James's students, and Dr. Samson Landmann, a follower of Theodore Meynert. In 1895, Pierce had published a critique of the results of Gurney, Janet, Alfred Binet, and others on the implications of post-hypnotic suggestion, entitled "Subliminal Self or Unconscious Cerebration?" and Frank Podmore, a member of the English Society for Psychical Research, had written a reply. James analyzed their criticisms, along with those of Dr. Albert von Schrenck-Notzing, practitioner of medicine in Munich, and Landmann, in the *Psychological Review* (1896), and concluded that none of the authors made any new contribution to the subject.

In Pierce's view, such phenomena as post-hypnotic suggestion are accounted for by the hypothesis of unconscious cerebration—the intelligent brain is habituated to certain simple behaviors, which are then perpetuated by so-called lower brain centers. Landmann believed that the brain functions simultaneously on three levels: self-consciousness, ideation and association without self-consciousness, and the so-called "sub-cortical centers," otherwise referred to as the unconscious. Simple reflexes and the performance of habitual tasks are likewise the function of these lower centers, leaving self-consciousness undisturbed. Both Pierce and Landmann subscribed to the so-called "searchlight view" of consciousness: that waking reality is somehow superior to other states of consciousness, and that knowledge of these other states comes when waking consciousness shines its most intelligent light down into the murky depths of the relatively dull and stupid domain of the unconscious.[11]

But Pierce and Landmann's view—that the secondary consciousness is a permanently inferior derivative of the primary one—says James, "is disproved by cases where a command given has to be intellectually worked out. Gurney has given his subjects problems in addition and multiplication. He has commanded them to write backwards; to count letters in a sentence; or to give an anecdote from their childhood. Meanwhile the subject might be either reading aloud, talking, or engaged in a conversation." The facts here suggest the operation of "two simultaneous conscious systems."

And we can see the same result in "Janet's case of Lucie, who counts signals up to 43" and then falls asleep, and who "multiplies 739 times 42." Here James's lecture notes refer to Pierre Janet's 1886 article, "Les Actes inconscients," or "Unconscious Acts and the Division of Personality under Induced Somnambulism." Lucie, Janet's patient, had been hypnotized and commanded to fall asleep when the hypnotizer's knocks reached 43. Then she was awakened, and while she performed various activities about the room, the hypnotizer began a series of knocks in an irregular fashion. At precisely 43 she fell asleep in an armchair. She asserted afterwards that during her period of activity she had heard the hypnotizer knock only once. Janet concluded that she must have been counting the remaining knocks, but unconsciously.

Janet verified this supposition with additional experiments. In one of them he commanded the subject while under hypnosis to multiply in writing 739 times 42. She was then awakened immediately. Her right hand wrote the numbers normally, performed the computation, and stopped when it was finished. Meanwhile, her attention was distracted toward the hypnotist, to whom she gave a detailed account of her daily activities. She remained oblivious of her right hand, not once looking at it while it wrote automatically.[12]

"As to whether or not mutually disconnected currents of conscious life can simultaneously exist in the same person," James's notes summarize, "the results show either split consciousness; *or* rapid alternations; *or* unconscious cerebration." None of these is really an unusual state of affairs, for "after all, [these theories] only reflect the development" of such routine and naturally occurring behaviors as the ability simultaneously to "walk and talk, or read aloud and think." We have here a whole "field of inattention."

It is at this point that James introduces what seemed to him the most plausible explanation for the existence of a secondary consciousness and one of the most important ideas presented in the lecture series—an idea on which many of his later interpretations were to hinge. This was F. W. H. Myers's formulation of "the subliminal consciousness." In his own publications, James referred continually to essays on the subliminal that Myers had published as a series in the early journals of the English Society for Psychical Research.[13]

In one specific issue drawing on James's own psychological language, Myers had said of the subliminal: "I suggest that the stream of consciousness in which we habitually live is not the only consciousness which exists in connection with our organism. Our habitual or empirical consciousness may consist of a mere selection from a multitude of thoughts and sensations, of which some at least are equally conscious with those that we empirically know. I accord no primacy to my ordinary waking self, except that among my potential selves this one has shown itself the fittest to meet the needs of common life. I hold that it has established no further claim, and that it is perfectly possible that other thoughts, feelings, and memories, either isolated or in continuous connection, may now be actively conscious, as we say, 'within me,'—in some kind of coordination with my organism, and forming some part of my total individuality. I conceive it possible that at some future time, under changed conditions, I may recollect all; I may assume the various personalities under one single consciousness, in which ultimate and complete consciousness, the empirical consciousness which at this moment directs my hand, may be only one element out of many."[14]

"Supraliminal" consciousness, that is, the everyday waking state, may be a mere extract of a greater reality, represented by all that is subliminal, or "transliminal," in the sense of consciousness "beyond the margin." Myers described this ultra-marginal reality in terms of varying grades across a psychic spectrum:

"At the inferior end, in the first place, it includes much that is too archaic, too rudimentary, to be retained in the supraliminal memory of an organism so advanced as man's. For the supraliminal memory of any organism is inevitably limited by the need of concentration of recollections useful in the struggle for existence. The recollection of processes now performed automatically, and needing no supervision, drops out from the supraliminal memory, but may be in my view retained in the subliminal. . . . In the second place, and at the superior or psychical end, the subliminal memory includes an unknown category of impressions which the supraliminal consciousness is incapable of receiving in any direct fashion, and which it must cognize, if at all, in the shape of messages from the subliminal consciousness."[15]

To this superior category Myers referred telepathic and clairvoyant impressions, which he believed to be habitually received not with the aid of those sensory operations that the supraliminal self commands directly but by operations peculiar to the subliminal self. This subliminal region, he maintained, functions according to laws unknown to waking consciousness, provides information in no clear way connected with the senses, and transcends the limitations of time and space as defined by rational consciousness.*

"We see a possible alternation between these two spheres," one conscious and the other subconscious, in "Barkworth's adding, and Dessoir's counting steps," James goes on to tell his audience. Here he was referring to the work of Thomas Barkworth, a member of the English Society for Psychical Research, and of Max Dessoir, a psychopathologist from Berlin. James cites an article by Barkworth in the Society's *Proceedings* entitled "Duplex Personality," in which many experiments were described that showed the working of arithmetic sums by the secondary intelligence. The subject was required to compute large numbers while in a hypnotized state. Later, in the waking state, the subject recorded his answers with a planchette (an automatic writing device consisting of a heart-shaped disc with three legs, one of which is a pencil; one or both hands resting on the disc will record, on a piece of paper, involuntary muscle movements as well as unconscious writing). The calculations were made correctly

---

* James himself had pointed out that manifestations from either end of the psychic spectrum could represent themselves to consciousness through the same channels, as when religious experiences are labeled psychotic, or diabolic elements of personality are given a divine interpretation. In light of such common misinterpretations, James said, our understanding of how to appeal to the intelligent, growth-oriented powers of the subconscious—knowing that the bestial, archaic part of our nature is always present—may be Myers's greatest contribution to the transformation of scientific psychology in the twentieth century.

by the automatic hand without the subject's awareness, since his attention was otherwise occupied at the time in reading aloud.[16]

James's notes also cite Dessoir's recent monograph, *Das Dopple Ich* (*The Double Ego,* 1889), and James's own copy of this work contains his marginal marks. Dessoir describes the ease with which the duality of thought and particularly its subconscious or underground dimension may be demonstrated. Dessoir used the normally automatic movements of walking as an example. He said that if we begin consciously to count our steps while walking, and at the same time pay complete attention to the events taking place around us on the street, within two weeks we will be able simultaneously to conduct a conversation and to say how many steps we have taken during the course of our walk. As a control, another person who does not participate in the conversation walks along counting the number of steps in order to verify the result. Dessoir then referred to Barkworth's development of this accomplishment. Diverted by a lively debate, Barkworth had been able to add long rows of numbers quickly and correctly. Dessoir suggested that this points not only to subconscious intelligence but also to subconscious memory.[17]

"But there are cases which look otherwise," James's notes remark. "Dessoir's observation" could be more like "the systematized anaesthesias in the case of Bernheim's described above," which may be nothing more than a split-off of fragments of the waking state. Yet we also have the case of "Miss X's crystal visions; is this split off? And what of Andrew Lang? And Morton Prince's case?"

James's review of Bernheim suggests that Bernheim considered hypnotically induced anaesthesias of the eye and ear as physiologically based in the cerebral hemispheres and the result of a splitting apart of the normally integrated functions of consciousness associated with sense perception. Separated from primary consciousness, these functions were mere inferior fragments. If this were the true state of affairs, however, then all instances of somnambulism would manifest this inferiority.

Yet, James asserts, that is not the case with the phenomenon of crystal vision exhibited by Miss X—actually Lucy Goodrich-Freer, who had written a number of articles on the subject for the *Proceedings of the English Society for Psychical Research* and published a book about her own apparently clairvoyant powers. A copy of Goodrich-Freer's book was in James's library. In his 1896 presidential address to the English Society for Psychical Research, "What Psychical Research Has Accomplished," published in *The Will to Believe* (1897), James reviewed her work briefly:

"One of the important experimental contributions [to psychical research] is the article of Miss X on Crystal Vision. Many persons who look fixedly into a crystal or other vaguely luminous surface fall into a kind of daze, and see visions. Miss X has this susceptibility in a remarkable degree, and is moreover, an unusually intelligent critic. She reports many visions which can only be described as apparently clairvoyant, and others which beautifully fill a vacant niche in our knowledge of subconscious mental operations. For example, looking into a crystal before breakfast one morning she reads in printed characters of the death of a lady of her acquaintance, the date and other circumstances all duly appearing in type. Startled by this, she looks at the *Times* of the previous day for verification, and there among the deaths are the identical words which she has seen. On the same page of the *Times* are other items which she remembers reading the day before: and the only explanation seems to be that her eyes then inattentively observed, so to speak, the death item, which forthwith fell into a special corner of her memory and came out as a visual hallucination when the peculiar modification of consciousness induced by the crystal-gazing set in."[18]

The facts are there, James suggests; but the interpretation

of whether they represent a separately existing and autono-
mous subliminal life or a mere fragment of the primary
waking state is still equivocal.* The question is whether
information received from secondary states of consciousness
is always derived in some way from previous experiences.
Those arguing against an independent secondary consciousness asserted that it was, while proponents of a theory like
Myers's continued to present evidence to the contrary. One
such proponent was Andrew Lang, who was a member of
the English Society for Psychical Research, although best
known as a folklorist and author of imaginative books of
fantasy for young readers.[19]

James had reviewed Lang's *Cock Lane and Common Sense*
and Carl du Prel's *Die Entdeckung der Seele durch die
Geheimwissenschaften (The Discovery of the Soul by Occult
Sources)*, in the *Psychological Review* (1894). There he
compared both to Myers's theory of the subliminal:

"Between Mr. Lang's facility in leaving things unsettled,
and Baron du Prel's facility in concluding them, it seems
as if a better path might be found. Might not the earnest
temper of science be combined somewhere with du Prel's
learning and the power of doubt of Lang? So far Mr. Myers's
papers on the 'Subliminal Self' seem to have kept nearest to

* Earlier, James had made a similar point in his review of A. Lalande's
Des Paramnesies for the *Psychological Review* (1 [1894], 94–95). Lalande had proposed a theory of déjà-vu or pre-vision—the common
illusion of feeling that one has already undergone some experience that
is occurring, has been with these very people in just this place, saying
just these things before, except that the experiences are all new and
often accompanied by strong emotion. James quoted Lalande as saying:
"The key to paramnesia must be sought in the existence of a double
perception, unconscious at first, then conscious." But whether this
comes from our unconscious perception that we at first experience
incompletely and then more fully register, or whether the perception
comes from sources actually independent of the perceiver, James left
open. At any rate, such perceptions obviously involve the deeper
recesses of the mind.

this idea, and both Lang's and du Prel's books set off by contrast the superiority of his work."[20]

James and Lang alike had submitted cases of subliminal phenomena to the English Society for Psychical Research, which were published together in 1895. Lang wrote: "A lady —not a nervous lady—was returning with her husband from a visit to the country. She lived in a kind of flat, above another house or tenement. In the train, on her journey, she expressed a firm belief that something dreadful had occurred at home. In fact, a servant had fallen through a glass cupola into a tenement beneath, and had killed herself. But the odd thing was that the maid's sister and a gentleman interested in the house where the accident had occurred both arrived before the ill news had reached them, both averring that they had been brought by nothing more than a vague presentiment of evil. So here were three coincident forebodings in one case, all fulfilled."[21] The case was corroborated by Myers.

In this instance, Lang's example raised the question of how three separate individuals could develop the same premonition for the outcome of events before they had even occurred. The information had not been known to waking consciousness beforehand and therefore could not be split off.

James then moves on to his third citation, the work of Morton Prince, a close friend and younger colleague in the Boston circle of psychotherapists. Originally trained in clinical medicine, Prince later turned his attention to diseases of the nervous system. At the time James delivered the Exceptional Mental States Lectures in 1896, Prince was teaching neurology at Harvard Medical School as an assistant to Professor James Jackson Putnam, another close friend of James's, who was chief of neurology at the Massachusetts General Hospital and also interested in the psychoneurosis.

We cannot be sure exactly which case of Prince's James is referring to here. Prince had published extensively on hypnosis, hysteria, and even some cases of crystal vision. Out of this work he constructed a major theory on the nature of ultra-marginal or, as Prince called them, co-conscious states of awareness.[22] James tells his audience of an example that Prince gave of messages from the subliminal whose content suggested that they were something more than merely split-off fragments of the waking state. Prince had first cited such an example in a paper read before the Suffolk Medical Society in 1886 entitled "Thought Transference." He recounted the case of the Reverend A. M. Creery, who had been practicing experiments with the "willing game" at home with his family, experiments that Prince reported were later more systematically verified by the English Society for Psychical Research.

Creery used himself, his four children, and his maid as subjects. One person would leave the room while the rest would select an object and all concentrate upon it; the person then reentered and attempted to name the object. After the first few trials, the successes preponderated and the capacity of the individual subjects at naming the thing the group had selected steadily increased to a high level of sophistication. They began with objects in the room, then chose names of towns, people, dates, cards out of a pack, lines of a poem— anything that the group could keep steadily before the mind. When in particularly good humor and excited about their successes, the children seldom made a mistake. Two elements were found to be of significance: the steadiness of concentration on a particular thought, and the intensity of willing it to pass to the mind of the subject making the guess.[23]

Prince maintained that the most important part of this demonstration was that it emphasized the active and willful part played by the persons whose thoughts are transferred, a point often lost sight of in most experiments. For James, these examples clearly pointed to the operation of a sub-waking secondary intelligence, both reflexive and psychic in nature. The farther reaches were completely unknown to current medical science, while the nearer reaches, at least, constituted the essential substrata of our forgotten memories, our dream images, our daily habits, and our philosophic attitudes.

"This leads to *automatism*," argues James, to "sensory and motor messages" from the subliminal. By automatism, James means physical or mental activity performed without awareness of the conscious self. He is referring particularly to the use of sensory and motor channels that express a secondary, but otherwise hidden, domain of personality. Sensory messages usually refer to visual, auditory, or kinesthetic hallucinations, whereas motor acts involve such behaviors as automatic writing, automatic talking, any form of spontaneous drawing, or other unconscious body movements. We recognize automatism most often in lower-level functioning of the nervous system; but it may also arise from elements of higher-level functioning that have become sufficiently isolated and in this condition show themselves in a crude and mechanical way. For whatever reason the fragment may be split off, it represents a line of communication between the higher and lower centers. Under hypnosis, for instance, if suggestion involves implanting an idea in the mind of a subject, then automatism most often characterizes the physical, motor, acting out of that idea.

Here James presents an array of examples that involve the transmission of information between the secondary and primary self of the same person, but whose source remains unknown to the primary self. His notes cite "Mrs. Shaler's case," "the Glines case," and the "Kettle case," but give no other details, except to suggest that they involved the technique of planchette writing. In vogue among the European and American well-to-do, the phenomenon of automatic writing received its impetus in the mid-nineteenth century from the activities of the spiritualists and mental healers. These practices were known to James early in his life, and he was to retain an interest in automatic writing throughout his career.[24]

"Planchette writing," his 1896 notes say, "makes Myers's notion [of an independently operating, intelligent, secondary consciousness] more plausible. . . . I have a whole drawer full" of these subliminal productions, "all varieties—mirror script, hieroglyphics, even the gift of tongues." And he notes that he should "read Albee, Underwood, Dean, and Saint Paul," as well as other examples, to his audience.

Though these names were drawn from memory (for the notes give no other annotations), some of the examples cited can still be traced. Helen R. Albee, for instance, wrote a popular book on mental healing, *The Gleam,* first published in 1911 by James's New York publisher, Henry Holt. In a chapter on psychic experiences, she recounted having overheard a friend talk about doing automatic writing. Although she had never tried the technique, she had known of it years earlier through the work of Charcot, Binet, James Sully, and the Society for Psychical Research. Miss Albee went straight home, put a pencil in her hand, and obeyed an impulse to write. At first nothing occurred; then the pencil became agitated, began to move rapidly and erratically, and at length wrote in the clear, ornamental hand of a sister who had died the previous year. Miss Albee then stated that Dr. William James quoted these communications in his classroom as an authentic and typical example of automatic writing.[25] Although undated, this initial experience is probably the one referred to by James in his lectures.

"Underwood" undoubtedly refers to the case of Mrs. Sarah Underwood described in the *Proceedings of the English Society for Psychical Research* in 1893 and detailed at greater length in Mrs. Underwood's book *Automatic or Spirit Writing,* published in 1896, a copy of which was in James's library. In the journal article, Mrs. Underwood told of a Mr. John Smith, an acquaintance of her husband's who had died more than a year earlier, leaving two daughters, Jennie and Violet. While waiting one night to begin automatic writing, with Mr. Underwood seated next to her by the fire reading and with no thought of Mr. Smith, Mrs. Underwood suddenly felt her pencil spring into action with the sentence: "John Smith will now enter into a conversation with B. F. Underwood."

Startled, Mr. Underwood leaned forward and questioned the "control" by asking it to verify the last time they had met before Smith's death. Smith reported the exact time, location, and circumstances. After a few more preliminary questions, Mr. Underwood asked through his wife if there was anything troubling Mr. Smith that he had forgotten to do before he died. Smith replied yes, to include his daughter Violet in his will. Some weeks later the Underwoods learned that Mr. Smith had indeed left Violet out of the will for marrying against his wishes. These facts were unknown to either Mr. or Mrs. Underwood until she received communication of them through automatic writing, and they were verified later by one of Mr. Smith's business associates.[26]

The earlier mention of hieroglyphics is connected with the reference to "Dean," actually the case of Sidney Dean, which James described in his "Notes on Automatic Writing" (1889), and again in 1890 in the *Principles*. James had said: "Mr. Sidney Dean of Warren, Rhode Island, was a member of congress from Connecticut from 1855 to 1859, a robust, active journalist and man of affairs, and for many years a writing subject who produced a large collection of manuscripts automatically written. 'Some of it,' he writes us, 'is in hieroglyph or strange compounded arbitrary characters, each series possessing a seeming unity in general design or character,' followed by what purports to be a translation or rendering into mother English. I never attempted the seemingly impossible feat of copying the characters. They were cut with the precision of an engraver's tool, and generally with a single rapid stroke of the pencil. Many languages, some obsolete and passed from history, are professedly given. To see them would satisfy you that no one could copy them except by tracing." They were also unidentifiable by any of James's

Harvard colleagues conversant with Sanskrit, Hebrew, Assyrian, Arabic, or the Kenji of Japan or China.[27]

As for "the gift of tongues," this refers to the quotation from St. Paul's Letter to the Corinthians, 4:19, in which he said: "I thank my God I speak with tongues more than ye all. Yet in the church I had rather speak five words with my own understanding than ten thousand in an unknown tongue," meaning that the language of tongues is an internal language intended to be used for inner transformation and for communication with the Divine. It is not the language of the marketplace.[28]

"All of which looks not like the triumph of any simple theory," remarks James; meaning that there is evidence both for and against the operation of a secondary consciousness that has true intelligence. He concludes with the statement that, in any event, "these phenomena appear to alternate between two spheres."

According to the newspaper accounts, James ended his lecture by pointing out that everyone could verify the reality of the subliminal for himself, if he were so interested. And he encouraged each person in his audience to experiment with the technique of automatic writing before the next lecture.[29]

HYSTERIA

James begins his third lecture with a recapitulation of
Myers's idea of the subliminal—that each person has within
him a simultaneous double consciousness. Above the threshold is everyday waking awareness, while below it are in-
numerable streams of consciousness. Some of these streams
Myers called dissolutive, others he called evolutive. But regardless of their nature—James tells his audience—the
operation of such streams distinctly "beyond the margin"
points to the reality of a subliminal consciousness.[1]

"I showed its presence," James comments, "in post-hypnotic
suggestion, in negative hallucinations, and in automatic
writing." His notes then mention the work of Herbert
Nichols, an instructor in psychology at Princeton, and
William Romaine Newbold, assistant professor of philosophy
at the University of Pennsylvania, both of whom had written
on intelligent unconscious reasoning.[2]

"Lately," the notion of a simultaneous double consciousness has been "applied to hysteria. My excuse for doing so,"
James's notes explain, "is that it sheds new light on our
mind's structure. It leads to a simple cure. And it converts a
dark chapter of human opinion into one relatively bright."
In short, the notes suggest, it is "optimistic!"

Hysteria, he continues, shows *"no definite symptoms."*
"Pains, insensibilities . . . palsy and contractions, unilateral
anaesthesias, fainting . . . loss of voice, hiccups, vomiting . . .
memories of inflammation . . . [of gums, of] joints, [instances
of] phlebitis, dyspepsia . . ." all "[are] quickly cured . . .[or]
come and go."

James had detailed the characteristics of hysteria some
years before in the *Principles,* saying: "One of the most constant symptoms in persons suffering from hysteric disease in
its extreme forms consists in alterations of the natural sensibility of various parts of the body. Usually the alteration is
in the direction of defects, or anaesthesia. One or both eyes
are blind, or color blind, or there is . . . blindness to one half
the field of view, or the field is contracted. Hearing, taste,
and smell may similarly disappear, in part or in totality. Still
more striking are the cutaneous anaesthesias. The old witch-
finders looking for the 'devil's seals' learned well the existence
of these insensible patches on the skin of their victims, to
which the minute physical examinations of modern medicine
have but recently again attracted attention. They may be
scattered anywhere but are very apt to affect one side of the
body. Not infrequently they affect an entire lateral half, from
head to foot, and the insensible skin of, say, the left side will
then be found separated from the naturally sensitive skin
of the right by a perfectly sharp line of demarcation down the
middle of the front and back. Sometimes, most remarkable
of all, the entire skin, hands, feet, face, everything, and the
mucous membranes, muscles and joints so far as they can be
explored, become completely insensible without the other
vital functions becoming gravely disturbed."[3]

The notes then mention "magnets, etc." in reference to
the influence of magnets and metals. In the *Principles,* James
had commented: "These hysterical anaesthesias can be made
to disappear more or less completely by various odd processes.
It has recently been found that magnets, plates of metal, or

the electrodes of a battery, placed against the skin, have this peculiar power. And when one side is relieved in this way, the anaesthesia is often found to have transferred itself to the opposite side, which until then was well. Whether these strange effects of magnets and metals be due to their direct physiological action, or to a prior effect on the patient's mind ('expectant attention' or 'suggestion') is still a moot question."[4]

These minor symptoms, he now continues, can sometimes culminate in "grave hysteria, with the full blown attacks," and precipitate a complete "unconsciousness therein." The French call this the stage of *attitudes passionnelles,* or "passionate attitudes," which suggests control of the field of consciousness by some single, powerful emotion. The term had been used to refer to the most severe stage of the hysterical crisis exhibited by violent contractions and paralysis.[5]

"Poor hysterics," comments James. "First they were treated as victims of sexual trouble . . . then of moral perversity and mediocrity . . . then of imagination. Among the various rehabilitations which our age has seen, none are more deserving or humane. It is a real disease, but a *mental* disease. It is a psychosis of a very peculiar kind," meaning only that it pertains to the mind, as against a *neurosis* or a condition of the nerves.

James then introduces his audience to the work of "Charcot's School." Jean-Martin Charcot was chief physician at the Salpêtrière Hospital in Paris, where Philippe Pinel earlier in the same century had freed the inmates from their chains and thus inaugurated a new age of enlightened care for the insane.[6]

Charcot initially made contributions in the field of neuropathology, then turned his attention to hysteria and epilepsy. He was a pioneer in the use of hypnosis as a scientific tool in France after it had been repeatedly denounced by scientific societies for more than a century. He also emphasized the prevalence of hysteria in males at a time when only women were thought to suffer from the disturbance. But the experiments he performed on the nature of functional paralysis remain his major contribution to psychology. Charcot was the first to demonstrate that hysterical paralysis was of psychic rather than physical origin. In the course of his work with patients at the Salpêtrière, Charcot noticed that hysterical cases would mimic the seizures of epileptics when the two kinds of disorders were confined in the same ward. No organic lesions or other causes could be found in his hysteric patients. Charcot then demonstrated with hypnotized subjects that each symptom of hysteria was the result of a subconscious fixed idea that could be traced back to its original cause, usually the memory of some traumatic experience. Hysteric patients could be easily hypnotized, and then, at the suggestion of the experimenter, be taken through what Charcot described as all the stages of the classical attack. Further, he found that hypnotized subjects would take on the symptoms of another patient when the two of them were brought into close proximity. Hysteria, Charcot concluded, was a disease of the mind without anatomical pathology.

Having introduced Charcot's work, James continues his discussion of anaesthesia: "Now this anaesthesia is very curious, and it was not until 1886 or thereabouts that its nature began to be cleared up, thanks to the observations of a number of French physicians"—that is, Charcot, Janet, Bernheim, and others. "It is an anaesthesia that comes and goes, an anaesthesia that gives the patient little trouble, an anaesthesia that is there only when the patient thinks about it, an anaesthesia that, in short, is not a genuine insensibility, but an insensitivity in certain relations and for certain purposes. Just the sort of defect that in olden times brought upon the whole class of hysteric subjects the accusation of being artful shammers and malingerers.

"Here for example, is a patient, the skin of whose whole side is supposed to be insensible. Lying with bandaged eyes, he is told to say 'yes' whenever he feels a pinch and 'no' when the pinch is unfelt, while the surgeon goes over his skin now here, now there, to test the power of sensation. To every pinch on the right side the patient replies 'yes' but whenever the left side is touched, instead of no reply at all being made (since it is anaesthetic) the patient says 'I feel nothing there.' But he must feel something in order to reply so opportunely.

"Here again is another patient who when her right eye is closed sees nothing, [because] her left eye is totally blind. By certain artifices it may be proved that this [left] eye sees perfectly when used along with the other. For instance, arm the patient with a pair of spectacles of which the right glass being red, stops all rays coming from green objects, making them invisible to the right eye which it covers. Then exhibit to the patient looking with both eyes, a prepared card on which are both green and red letters. The patient reads them all, she must therefore have used her left eye, for the right eye cannot possibly see the red letters. Similarly, hold a prism before her right eye, both of her eyes being open. She will forthwith say that she sees double, an effort optically impossible unless both eyes be simultaneously used."[7] In another example, a partially blind subject, when unexpectedly thrown a ball in the hospital yard, was able to catch it with no disturbance of coordination.

It seems, continues James, "like an elective anaesthesia," and he then cites different classes of objects that a subject might be electively sensitive or insensitive to: "a hairpin, earrings, a lock of hair, scissors, a match, a mouse." James's lecture notes show that he was referring to Pierre Janet's discussion of systematized or elective anaesthesias in *L'Automatisme psychologique*. In James's copy of that work a number of unusual observations are marked in which a subject appears at first to be totally anaesthetic to all objects, but then exhibits sensibility for only certain items.

One such subject, M., could not feel any object placed in her hand, yet she could reach up and feel the presence or absence of her gold earrings, her wedding ring, or her gold hairpin. Janet thought that gold metal was the common element, so he handed M. a gold piece which, because her hands were completely anaesthetic, she did not feel. But as soon as the coin was placed in her hand, she immediately reached up and touched one of her gold earrings and checked to see if her hairpin was in place.[8]

Another hysteric subject, Lucie, would awaken in the middle of the night, light her lamp, and proceed furiously with the house cleaning, which she could not do during the day. Once when someone holding a lighted lamp followed her and tried to get her attention, Lucie failed to react in any way to the person's voice or gestures. But when her own lamp began to falter, she attended to it immediately. Lucie's anaesthesia extended only to those objects to which she elected to pay no attention. When she carried her own lamp, she would attend to no others. Regardless of the number of lamps in the room, she would call it completely dark if hers was unlit. Janet observed some instances in which Lucie was influenced by the other lights, but if she saw them, she always assumed that they were her own. If one of the other lamps faltered and began to go out, she would merely turn her own lamp up a bit.[9]

Janet reported a similar instance of a man holding a match. No matter how many matches were lit, he saw only his match. Similarly, a subject whose senses were totally anaesthetic could be handed a pair of scissors or a mouse and hold either in the appropriate manner, but still assert that he felt nothing and held nothing.

"Is this shamming?" James asks. "No! It is just like the hypnotically suggested anaesthesias of last time, where Bernheim says 'You can hear,' where the patient is made to remember what she didn't feel, where she must single out a particular line on a blackboard in order not to see it. Not a sensorial but an intellectual blindness is suggested here from within. The mind is split into two parts. One part agrees not to see anything with the left eye alone," while the other sees with the right eye perfectly well.

James then mentions English and French studies examining the possibility that such hysterical phenomena could be "self-suggested." Charcot had pointed this out first, and Janet, Binet, Bernheim, Myers, and others had concurred. Hypnosis, they all agreed, was obviously the implantation of suggestion by others, whereas hysteria involved a repetitive or otherwise convincing suggestion upon oneself. Of this alleged disability of the subject, Myers had commented: "The essential character of hysteria is an unreasonable autosuggestion in regions of the mind which are below the power of normal consciousness, *beyond the powers of the waking will.* . . . Hysteria is a malady of the hypnotic layer, *a disease of the hypnotic stratum.*"[10]

The implications here were important for the progress of psychotherapy, for they meant that hysteric symptoms arose out of a choice the patient had made at an earlier time to avoid painful or traumatic memories. For whatever reason, at some highly suggestive moment the subject seeded the hypnotic layer with self-suggested memories that then became inaccessible to waking consciousness.

James's notes give some examples: "Janet finds memories of pictures shown to the blind eye come back when sensibility is restored—a serpent, a tree . . . just as in the hypnotic cases mentioned last time." He is referring to another example cited by Janet in *L'Automatisme psychologique*, in which the hysteric subject Marie kept her good right eye closed, while Janet passed a simple drawing of a tree with a serpent wrapped around it in front of the hysterically blind left eye. The drawing was then hidden away and Marie opened her good right eye. She asserted she had seen nothing.

But Janet recounted that when he applied a favorite piece of iron against Marie's temple, it purportedly restored sight to the hysterically blind eye, and with it memory of the stimulus originally reported as not having been seen.[11] Janet concluded that anaesthesia for a certain object abolished memory for that class of objects; and that when sensitivity returned, so did all prior memory, including memory of the stimulation applied while anaesthetized.

"Something sees and feels in the person, but the waking self of the person does not," James concludes. "That something might be hyper-aesthetic." Here he is referring to another of the most common symptoms of hysteria, the exalted sensibility of the secondary intelligence. The subliminal stratum is supersensitive, and even the weakest stimuli are experienced with great intensity. Normally inaudible sounds are clearly heard; distant objects can be seen in clearer detail than usual; faint heat or cold applied to the skin is felt as extreme. In hysteria, as in hypnosis, the hypnotic stratum is overexposed. This may account for what Janet witnessed in his patients.

As if to shed light on this problem, James's notes next introduce an extensive series of experiments by Alfred Binet, colleague of Charcot and Janet, who had studied hypnotism and multiple personality before turning his attention to the measurement of intelligence in young children. James refers to passages out of Binet's *Les Altérations de la personalité*; his own copy of the work contains an inscription by Binet, James's signature, and James's extensive marginal markings, which correspond to references in the Exceptional Mental States lecture notes.[12]

Binet pointed out that in hysterical subjects the threshold of consciousness has only a relative value and may shift with different states of consciousness. There is no such thing as an absolute threshold, as the German psychophysicists believed. The unprecedented assumption of a "nothing" beyond the measured threshold may reflect only the inability of waking consciousness to project itself into states of subwaking intelligence.[13]

Binet showed that the unconscious sensibility of hysteric subjects is at times much more acute than in normal subjects. For example, the hysteric subjects were able to draw accurately the inscription of a small coin that had been placed on the back of their neck.[14] By placing a chart of letters at a distance so that the seeing eye of a hysteric subject could not read the bottom lines, he demonstrated that where normal vision leaves off, subliminal vision begins. When the bottom lines were shown to the subject's blind eye, the subject reported seeing nothing, but by automatic writing wrote even the smallest lines of letters correctly.[15] Binet also showed that subconscious stimulation can influence conscious judgments. A hysteric subject's anaesthetized hand was placed behind a screen and pricked nine times. The subject reported that he felt nothing; but when asked to choose any number at random, he always chose the number of times his insensible hand had just been pricked.[16]

"So with Janet's case of Lucie with papers in her lap," James's notes continue, "made post-hypnotically blind to certain ones which by automatic writing she says she sees. Her hand and arm sensibility are tested in the same way." Janet's famous case of Lucie, the nineteen-year-old hysteric patient he had first observed at Le Havre and then written about in the *Revue philosophique,* had already been cited by James in the *Principles* and elsewhere.

In Lucie's trance Janet covered her lap with cards, each bearing a number. He then told her that on waking she would not be able to see any card whose number was a multiple of 3. Accordingly, when she was awakened and asked to identify the papers in her lap, she counted and named only those whose number was not a multiple of 3. But her hand, when the subconscious self was interrogated by the usual method of engrossing the upper self in another conversation, wrote that the only cards in Lucie's lap were

those numbered 12, 18, 9, and so on; and when asked to pick
up all the cards that were there, she picked up these and let
the others lie.

The anaesthesias, paralyses, contractions, and other irregu-
larities from which hysterics suffer, James concludes, seem
then due to the fact that their secondary personage has en-
riched itself by robbing the primary one of a function which
the latter ought to have retained.[17] James sums up: "Consciousness splits, and two halves share the field." In hysteria
as well as in hypnosis, the total functions of the normally
intact personality seem parceled out between the different
selves of the person.

He compares this phenomenon in hysterics to the automatism exhibited in growing children, citing in his notes
Binet's case of Marguerite. "Armande" and "Marguerite"
were the names Binet adopted to disguise the identity of his
two daughters, who were the subjects of his published observations on child development made after 1890.[18]

For instance, Binet was able to develop a reflex reaction
in his infant daughter. When he stroked her outstretched
palm, her fingers would curl up; and when he stroked the
closed hand, he could then make it open. He succeeded in
getting the same reaction when she was awake or asleep, or
when her attention was distracted elsewhere. Binet noted
the ease with which he was also able to evoke other more
highly coordinated movements from the young child when
her attention was distracted. Yet these were movements that
the child could not yet carry out voluntarily. He also observed instances in which two distinct mental states exist at
the same time but mutually expel each other and never
mingle. It would be difficult to find such clear phenomena of
mental disaggregation in adults, Binet said, except of course
in hysteria, and other analogous conditions.

"[Hysterics] are not shammers then," James concludes.
"But how does such splitting come to pass?" He answers by
summarizing the different views then prevailing among

French and German pioneers in the psychotherapy of the subconscious. "Janet says it is from a synthetic weakness" of the will. "[Josef] Breuer says the weakness is due to splitting. . . . The question, [however, is still] open."*

The essence of hysteria appears, as Breuer put it, to be the influence of a traumatic shock isolating consciousness from a part of itself, rather than a weakening of the barrier between consciousness and other possible states already existent below the threshold, as Janet believed.[19]

"Anyhow," James's notes continue, "a shock often starts [the hysterical cycle], and here comes the interesting chapter,

---

* James was referring here to a very important historical sequence of events that began in the mid-1880s, at the time Freud was first acquainting himself with Charcot. By then, Janet's work with hysterical patients had already caused a sensation in Charcot's circle. Janet first published his results in the *Revue philosophique*. Later, his articles culminated in the appearance of his Ph.D. dissertation, *L'Automatisme psychologique*, in 1889, the same year that James, Janet, Freud, and others attended the International Congress of Experimental Psychology in Paris. Breuer and Freud then published their *Uber den Psychischen Mechanismus Hysterischer Phänomene* (1893), which acknowledged close similarity with Janet's work. Janet's dissertation for the M.D., *Etat mental des hystériques,* came out in 1894 and contained a critique of, among others, Breuer and Freud's interpretation of hysterical mechanisms. In 1895 Breuer and Freud published their *Studien über Hysterie,* in which Breuer reviewed Janet's interpretation.

A somewhat heated controversy followed. Janet reviewed *Studien über Hysterie,* saying: "I am happy to see that the results of my already old findings have been recently confirmed by two German authors, Breuer and Freud." By 1896 Freud had broken with Breuer and had followed with a series of papers showing his differences with Janet—differences that later proved to be far fewer than Freud had originally suggested.

For a provocative comparison of Freud and Janet, see Henri Ellenberger, *Discovery of the Unconscious* (New York: Basic Books, 1970), p. 539; for an excellent but opposite view of these developments from a psychoanalytic standpoint, see Kenneth Levin, *Freud's Early Psychology of the Neuroses: A Historical Perspective* (Pittsburgh: University of Pittsburgh Press, 1978).

as in Janet, Breuer, [or] Freud, [the] memory of the shock becomes subconscious, and parasitic." In an article for the *Psychological Review,* James had remarked of this process in 1894: "The weakness in question is described by M. Janet substantially as follows. In the constitution called hysterical the threshold of the principal consciousness is not fixed, but movable. It can be shifted by physical and moral shocks and strains so that sensations and ideas of which the patient ought to be fully aware become 'subliminal,' or buried and forgotten, and in this parasitic state persist more or less monotonously. The nucleus of these subconscious fixed ideas usually consists of reminiscences of the shock by which the mind was originally shattered; but in process of time other painful reminiscences may be added, and accidental associations may complicate the system which, from its hiding place below the principal consciousness, may produce effects eruptive (hallucinations and motor impulses) as well as subtractive (anaesthesias, abulias [will-lessness], confusions, etc.) and moreover may influence the bodily functions in manifold and formidable ways."[20]

In other words, the traumatic memory of the shock, being too anxiety-provoking for the waking self to bear, becomes dissociated and is taken over by the secondary consciousness. The forgotten memory then takes on the power of a fixed idea. Once the idea is the property of the subconscious, it attracts to itself other forgotten, anxiety-provoking memories that are of similar content. The fixed idea in truth grows into a complex constellation of memories that is beyond the control of waking consciousness, but the presence of which is expressed in the characteristics of the hysteric attack or as a symptom of organic disease.

And of Breuer and Freud's view of the nature of hysteria, James said in the same review: "Hysteria for them starts always from a shock, and is a 'disease of the memory.' Certain reminiscences of the shock fall into the subliminal consciousness, where they can only be discovered in 'hypnoid' states. If left there, they act as permanent psychic traumata, thorns in the spirit, so to speak."[21]

"Often a regular *collection* of such ideas can be *tapped* in hypnosis, dreams, and automatic writing attacks," James now tells his audience. In 1894 he had commented on this:

"M. Janet proves the existence of these fixed ideas by many methods, by hypnosis, by automatic writing, by the hallucinations that come out in 'crystal gazing,' by the patient's talk during sleep, by utterances during the attack, and finally by what he calls 'the method of distraction,' which practically is only a variety of automatic writing. In these circumstances hysterics will reveal obsessive memories and ideas of which their principal consciousness is wholly unaware, and will explain in detail the images by which their various symptoms are determined."[22]

Now James's lecture notes refer to "Breuer's method of mere talk-cure," which James himself had described in 1894: "The cure is to draw the psychic traumata out in hypnotism, let them produce all their emotional effects, however violent, and *work themselves off.* They make then (apparently) a new connection with the principal consciousness, whose breach is thus restored and the sufferer gets well."[23]

The "talk-cure" and "chimney sweeping" were the names given to Breuer's therapeutic method by his famous patient Anna O., who was later identified by Ernest Jones, Freud's biographer, as Bertha Pappenheim. The cure involved discovery of the fixed idea under hypnosis and then presentation of that idea to the patient in a relaxed but normal waking condition. The effect was to make the person relive the experience by calling forth the forgotten idea and the intense emotions associated with it. Once the idea was acknowledged by the patient's waking consciousness and emotional expression given its full vent, the hysterical symptoms disappeared.

James concludes his presentation by reporting on six cases

treated successfully by Janet, and one by Breuer and Freud. In each instance, external symptoms were traced to subliminal fixed ideas.

First, the lecture notes cite Justine, a patient of Janet's who had a morbid fear of cholera, which Janet traced to a traumatic episode. James had written about the case in the *Psychological Review* (1894) in a notice of Janet's article "Histoire d'une Idée Fixe":

". . . Justine, a woman of forty, of psychopathic heredity, who from early childhood had had fears and spasmodic attacks, and who, at the age of seventeen, in consequence of having assisted in the 'laying out' of two cholera patients, was seized with a haunting fear of this disease, which in three years made her a wreck. Her worst feature consisted in frequent convulsive attacks of dread of the cholera, with vomiting, purging, and hallucinations of every sense. This condition had already lasted twenty years when Janet first saw the patient. The treatment consisted first in altering, by suggestions made during the attacks, now one and then another element of the terrifying hallucinations, until their whole character was changed. This cured the attacks; but the original state of waking *choleraphobia* returned. M. Janet found that the nucleus of this emotion was the insistent presence of the *word* 'cholera' on the lips, as a phenomenon of motor automatism. He soon transformed the obsessive word as he had transformed the more complete hallucinations of the attack, by substituting other syllables, making chocolate, coqueluche, cocoriko, etc. The chronic state of fear departed with the dreadful word; but all sorts of other morbid ideas and impulses then showed themselves, partly due to accidental suggestions, and each easily cured by counter-suggestion, but each presently succeeded by another, so that the woman's condition remained on the whole deplorably abnormal. From this state of suggestibility, abulia, and scatter-wittedness he rescued her by a year of pedagogic training, gymnastic and intellectual. His patience must have been great, for the whole narrative of treatment covers three years."[24]

Next, James's notes cite Isabella and Marcella, who were both mentioned in his 1894 review of Janet: "Isabella cannot eat," James had said there. "She knows not why, but it appears that during each of her 'attacks' her dead mother appears to her, upbraids her for a past misdemeanor, calls her unworthy to live, and forbids her to take food. . . . Similarly, Marcella's anorexia comes from a voice which she hears during her attacks and which orders her to starve."[25]

Gib, another of Janet's patients whom James describes to his audience, fell ill on learning of the death of her niece, who had thrown herself out of a window in a fit of delirium. First Gib had ecstasies thinking of the niece; then more restless dreams, accompanied by motions in which she tried to throw herself out of a window. She developed somnambulisms and attacks of convulsion, evidently induced by the emotion that this painful recollection awakened in her enfeebled mind. After trying to throw herself from a window, she became sad, preoccupied, unable to do any work or give her attention to anything, and she claimed not to know what troubled her. Yet when she had a pencil in her hand, she scribbled at random on bits of paper and in these formless marks one could recognize the design of a window and the name of the niece.[26]

James also summarizes the dynamics of "Vel's tic," again described in the 1894 review of Janet: "Vel . . . for eight years had had a particularly odious tic, consisting in an expulsion of air through the nose, and a contortion of one side of the face. This resists every conceivable treatment, for the patient's consciousness is irresistible and motiveless. The moment he is hypnotized, however, he says, '*j'ai une croûte dans le nez; elle me gêne*'; and a corrective suggestion then made abolished the symptom. It would appear that the subconscious delusion here dated from certain nose bleeds in a typhoid fever eight years before."[27]

James then gives his audience an account of the case of
Marie, the sixth of Janet's patients. In an earlier detailed
article of 1890 entitled "The Hidden Self," James had
described Janet's method of treatment with this patient:

"Marie came to the hospital . . . with monthly convulsive
crises, chill, fever, delirium, and attacks of terror lasting
for days, together with various shifting anaesthesias and con-
tractures all the time, and a fixed blindness of the left eye. At
first M. Janet took little interest in the patient, divining no
particular psychological factor in the case. She remained in
the hospital for seven months, and had all the usual course
of treatment applied, including water cure and ordinary
hypnotic suggestions, without the slightest good effect.

"Then she fell into a sort of despair, of which the result
was to make M. Janet try to throw her into a deeper trance,
so as to get, if possible, some knowledge of the original causes
of the disease, of which, in the waking state and in ordinary
hypnotism, she could give no definite account. He succeeded
even beyond his expectations; for both her early memories
and the internal memory of her crises returned in the deep
somnambulism, and she explained three things: Her periodic
chill, fever, and delirium were due to a foolish immersion
of herself in cold water at the age of thirteen. The chill, fever,
etc., were consequences which then ensued; and now, years
later, the experience then stamped in upon the brain for the
first time was repeating *itself* at regular intervals in the form
of an hallucination undergone by the subconscious self, and
of which the primary personality only experienced the outer
results. . . .

"The attacks of terror were accounted for by another
shocking experience. At the age of sixteen she had seen an old
woman killed by falling from a height; and the subconscious
self, for reasons best known to itself, saw fit to believe itself
present at this experience also whenever the other crises came
on. The hysterical blindness of her left eye had the same sort
of origin, dating back to her sixth year, when she had been

forced, in spite of her cries, to sleep in the same bed with another child, the left half of whose face bore a disgusting eruption. The result was an eruption on the same parts of her own face, which came back for several years before it disappeared entirely, and left behind it an anaesthesia of the skin and blindness of the eye.

"So much for the origin of the poor girl's various afflictions. Now for the cure! The thing needed, of course, was to get the subconscious personality to leave off having these senseless hallucinations. But they had become so stereotyped and habitual that this proved no easy task to achieve. Simple commands were fruitless; but M. Janet at last hit upon an artifice, which shows how many resources the successful mind-doctor must possess. He carried the poor Marie back in imagination to the earlier dates. It proved as easy with her as with many others when entranced, to produce the hallucination that she was again a child, all that was needed being an impressive affirmation to that effect. Accordingly, M. Janet, replacing her in this wise at the age of six, made her go through the bed scene again, but gave it a different *dénouement.* He made her believe that the horrible child had no eruption and was charming, so that she was finally convinced, and caressed without fear this new object of her imagination. He made her re-enact the scene of the cold immersion, but he gave it also an entirely different result. He made her live again through the old woman's accident, but substituted a comical issue for the old tragical one which had made so deep an impression. The subconscious Marie, passive and docile as usual, adopted these new versions of the old tales; and apparently was either living in monotonous contemplation of them or had become extinct altogether when M. Janet wrote his book [1889]. For all morbid symptoms ceased as if by magic. 'It is five months,' our author says, 'since these experiments were performed. Marie shows no longer the slightest mark of hysteria. She is well; and in particular, has grown quite stout. Her physical aspect

has absolutely changed.' Finally, she is no longer hypnotizable, as often happens in these cases when the health returns."[28]

Last, James's lecture notes cite "Breuer's Lucy," which is
presumably Freud's case of Miss Lucy R. Breuer does not
appear to have mentioned a case of Lucy that he himself
treated. On the other hand, in James's copy of *Studien über
Hysterie* the case of Miss Lucy R. is marked frequently with
his characteristic pencil strokes, and it is the only case,
except for Breuer's Anna O., so marked in the book.

Miss Lucy R., a young governess suffering from hallucinations while recovering from suppurative rhinitis, came to
Freud through a colleague in 1892. She was suffering from
depression and fatigue and was tormented by subjective
sensations of "the smell of burnt pudding." The interior of
her nose was completely analgesic and without reflexes, but
there was no loss of tactile sensibility and no restriction in
the visual field. Freud treated the olfactory hallucination as
a chronic hysterical symptom and assumed that her depression
might be the affect attaching to the trauma; his attempts at
inducing hypnotic somnambulism were unsuccessful. She
would remain only in a light state of suggestibility, without
moving hand or foot, quietly resting, eyes closed.

Freud asked her if she could remember the occasion on
which she had first experienced the smell of burnt pudding.
She replied in this light trance that she knew exactly, and
recounted an incident that had occurred to her two months
ago, prior to her therapy, which was two days before her
birthday. A governess, she was with the children in the
schoolroom playing at cooking. A letter suddenly arrived
for her from her mother in Glasgow, but the children rushed
toward her and grabbed it, shouting, "No, you must wait to
open it until your birthday." While the children played this
game with her, she suddenly smelled burnt pudding, which
they had forgotten on the stove. Ever since then Lucy had
been persecuted by this smell.

Freud was not satisfied with this explanation, feeling that the hysterical idea must be intentionally repressed from consciousness in order to exert an unconscious effect. He challenged the governess to admit that the real conflict was that she was in love with her employer. The smell of burnt pudding then disappeared as a symptom, only to be replaced by the hallucinatory smell of cigar smoke. Getting the patient to visualize the related memory, Freud discovered that cigar smoke had been present at a disagreeable scene in which the children's father had reprimanded an old family friend for kissing his children on the mouth, and then turned on Lucy, the governess, as someone to blame for permitting such disgusting behavior, threatening dismissal if she let such acts persist. The incident involving the cigar smell had occurred earlier than the burnt pudding incident, and therefore, Freud reasoned, was the more traumatic and deeply imbedded of the two. Eliminating the repression of the burnt pudding incident revealed the deeper repression of the cigar smoke.

The result of these admissions on the part of the patient was an end of the depression and sadness, and a return of normal sensibility to the previously anaesthetized interior of the nose.[29]

So we see, says James in conclusion, that "subconscious fixed ideas can have their effect," and there are "not sole types" of hysteric personalities. His notes for this lecture end with what appears to be a final quotation: "From these depths, etc. . . ."—suggesting that with such discoveries comes "new hope for insane delusions." The quotation has not been recovered. However, James did provide a concluding statement to his ideas on hysteria in an alternate set of lecture notes. It reads:

"But the enigmatic character of much of all this cannot be contested, even though there is a deep and laudable desire of the intellect to think of the world as existing in a clean and regular shape. The mass of literature growing more abundant daily, from which I have drawn my examples, consisting as it does almost exclusively of oddities and eccentricities, of grotesqueries and masqueradings, incoherent, fitful, personal, is certainly ill-calculated to bring satisfaction either to the ordinary medical mind or that of a psychological turn. The former has its cut and dried classifications and routine therapeutic appliances of a material order; the latter has its neat notions of the cognitive and active powers, its laws of association and the rest. Everything here is so lawless and individualized that it is chaos come again; and the dramatic and humoring and humbugging relation of operator to patient in the whole business is profoundly distasteful to the orderly characters who fortunately in every profession most abound. Such persons don't wish a *wild* world, where tomfoolery seems as if it were among the elemental and primal forces. They are perfectly willing to let such exceptions go unnoticed and unrecorded. They are in too bad form for scientific recognition. So the universe of fact starts with the simplest of all divisions, the respectable and academic system, and the mere delusions. Thus is the orderliness which is the general desideratum, gained for contemplation."[30] He rightly saw that in the concrete world of raw experience, order was actually the exception rather than the rule.

: LECTURE IV :
MULTIPLE
PERSONALITY

"We are by this time familiar with the notion that a man's consciousness need not be a fully integrated thing," James begins this fourth lecture. "From the ordinary focus and margin, from the ordinary abstraction, we shade off into phenomena that look like consciousness *beyond the margin.* Hypnotism and automatic writing have been our means of approach. In the relief of certain hysterics, by handling the buried idea—whether as in Freud . . . or in Janet, we see a portent of the possible usefulness of these new discoveries. The awful becomes relatively trivial.

"But we must pass now to cases where the division of personality is more obvious." His notes then quote a brief Latin phrase, *"alienate a se,"* that is, alienation from one's self, a condition known since the classical philosophers. "Of late years," he points out, we have seen "many cases of *alternating* personality." The notes go on to list three types in particular: "fugues," the passage from one state of consciousness into another with complete loss of memory for the previous state; "epileptic cases," the convulsive fits, contractions, and anaesthesia of the hysterical crisis, which pass off when the subject returns to the waking state; and "psychopathic cases and dreamy states," meaning instances of morbid insanity, accompanied by transient hallucinatory experiences such as dreaming, but which occur while fully conscious.[1]

All such states were considered pathological from a medical standpoint. To them James adds a "fourth type, mediumship," in which he suggests the possibility of a benign, psychic, even transcendent dimension of personality. He then enumerates some examples.

As a class, the four types of alternating personality all appear to be instances of ambulatory automatism; that is, coordinated action which the person performed while in somnambulistic sleep. The various states James describes always *alternate* with each other. He introduces "Tissié's case" of Albert, "Raymond's case of P.," and "mine of Miss O."

Philippe Tissié, whose work James cited in the first lecture, had described Albert in his monograph *Les Aliénés voyageurs* (1887), and again in the later book, *Les Rêves* (1890), on dreams and related states. We cannot be sure which one James is quoting from, but Tissié's work was widely cited by Charcot's school in France, and by many researchers associated with the loose-knit Boston School of Psychotherapy in America at the end of the nineteenth century.

Albert had come to the attention of medical authorities as an adult after he was found wandering around in a delirious state, without identification and unable to give any account of himself. Tissié reports that Albert had fallen out of a tree when he was eight years old, plunging down and sustaining a severe concussion. After a period of apparent recovery from the accident, his behavior became unusual. At the age of twelve, while working at a local gas company, he went off on an errand one day and never returned. Some months later he was discovered working for an umbrella merchant. His brother, whom he did not recognize, came to fetch him, and it took a sharp slap on the face for Albert to snap out of his amnesia. Quite to his own surprise, he recovered his former identity.

He returned to his old job, but every few months would go off into a "fugue." He would wake up in an unknown place and have to ask where he was; often he found himself in jail, under arrest for lack of identity papers. Thinking to alleviate his problem, Albert enlisted in the army. But he immediately began to wet the bed and had a return of the intense migraine headaches he had suffered just after the original accident; he also developed intermittent fever, severe diarrhea, and other symptoms. He became a compulsive walker, always in a straight line. One day while marching, his group was spread out over the terrain and veered to one side, but Albert kept walking in a straight line. On that occasion he walked halfway across Europe.[2]

"Raymond's case of P." refers to a case of double consciousness reported by Professor Fulgence Raymond, a neurologist who succeeded Charcot at the Salpêtrière in 1893. Raymond allowed Janet to continue the pursuit of Charcot's interest in traumatic neurosis, publishing jointly with him throughout the 1890s. The case of P. was first described in 1895 by Raymond and Janet, and by Raymond again in his *Maladies du système nerveux* (1896). It was another instance of ambulatory automatism.[3]

P. had been brought to the Salpêtrière Hospital after he had disappeared from his home in Nancy and awakened eight days later lying in the snow by the train tracks in Brussels. Raymond and Janet eventually discovered that the man had a morbid background. P.'s troubles began when he was falsely accused of theft at the age of sixteen. He became crazed for several hours, and the episode was followed by recurring violent headaches. He left home a year later, endured a traumatic experience, and developed nightmares. The guilt stemming from the false accusation became combined with the terrors he experienced in fleeing his home.

Finally he left for South America. Working for the famous French explorer Jules Crevaux, he narrowly escaped an Indian massacre. Upon his return to France, P. joined another expedition to Africa, where he became ill from various causes, particularly marsh fever. He brought the sickness back to Europe, but eventually recovered. He was married, but his wife died within three months. Desperation set in and he tried to enlist in the army, but his family intervened. Two years later he married again, this time happily. The second marriage produced two children. He established a modest business, took on extra work as an accountant, and also began publishing a study he had made of the flora and fauna of Africa and South America.

But within a few years P. became subject to nervous troubles from overwork, developed cramps, trembling, and spots in front of his eyes, and showed a diminished aptitude for work. He grew easily distracted, began to lose his mobility, and his emotions became highly exaggerated.

One night while his wife was away, P. started for home after drinking with some friends. He distinctly remembered all the details leading to crossing a bridge within sight of his house. Halfway across the bridge he lost all memory of subsequent events. Eight days later he was found in Belgium. Only by the use of extensive therapeutic methods were Raymond and Janet able to get P. to recover his memory for the events of this blank period. Except by such therapeutic methods, alternation of personality with subsequent loss of memory seemed to be the rule in these cases.

James's own case, "mine of Miss O.," may refer to one of the few patients he took into his home for treatment. We know only that these cases were melancholics—in other words, they suffered from depression—and that at least one of them left successfully cured. But there is no corroborating evidence that any of these was Miss O. He did see other patients, one of whom was certainly a case of alternating personality. That instance, the case of Ansel Bourne, which we will soon describe, was a subject in an experiment on hypnosis and automatic writing that James specifically said he conducted for therapeutic purposes.

Accounts also exist of James's referral of patients with mental problems to psychic healers, who attempted their own kind of cure under James's supervision. And there is the case of James's sister, Alice, who was prone to severe hysteric attacks up to her death in 1892; in fact, Alice identified herself with several cases of alternating personality that James had described in his 1890 essay on "The Hidden Self." We do not know whether one of these may have described Miss O. It is clear, however, that James is referring to an instance of multiple personality, probably another case of ambulatory automatism, that he himself had treated.[4]

James then broaches the possibility that not all instances of alternating personality are "hysteric cases." As an example he describes the experiences of Mary Reynolds, whose case was originally brought to light by Dr. John Kearsley Mitchell in the 1830s and published in 1888 by his son, Silas Weir Mitchell, distinguished Philadelphia neurologist, literary figure, and a pioneer in the rest and diet treatment of nervous disorders.[5]

In the *Principles,* James had described Mary Reynolds as a dull and melancholy young woman living in the Pennsylvania wilderness in 1811. One morning, long after her usual time of rising, she was found in a deep sleep from which she could not be awakened. After twenty hours she awakened by herself, but in an unnatural state of consciousness. She had no memory and could not speak, except for a few words uttered instinctively, unrelated to any coherent ideas. She did not recognize her family or friends, and was not aware that they were in any way related to her. The house, the fields, the forest, the hills, valleys, and streams, all were new and unexplored. She appeared as if an infant just born, yet in a state of maturity. Her personality became dramatically changed. Originally melancholy and taciturn, she became cheerful, buoyant, even a trickster, and she was much more socially active, although she acted as if among strangers.

This change went on for five weeks until one morning, after a protracted sleep, Mary awoke as her former self. She immediately recognized her family and friends, and returned unhesitatingly to her former duties. She retained no memory whatsoever of her activities of the previous five weeks—her forest trips, her humor and tricks all faded completely from memory. She had no knowledge of any new acquisitions she had made. She again became melancholy and even more deeply withdrawn, although her family was most relieved, believing the interim episodes to be gone for good. In a few weeks, however, she again fell into a profound sleep and awoke in her second state, taking up the new life where she had left off. The two periods, widely separated, were to her as but one night.

These alternations from one state to another continued at intervals of varying length for fifteen or sixteen years. They finally ceased when she reached the age of thirty-six, leaving her permanently in her second state, which continued for the last quarter century of her life. Mary Reynolds developed from a gay, hysterical, mischievous person into a joyful, loving, social woman whose actions were tempered by sober usefulness. She seemed well balanced and showed no ill effect from the change that had taken place, although occasionally she would have a shadowy dream of a dim past. She died peacefully in the home of her nephew, the Reverend John Reynolds, in January 1854 at the age of sixty-one.[6]

James next presents another case of ambulatory automatism in which the subject under hypnosis had been able successfully to regain the memory of his lost wanderings. This was the case (mentioned earlier) of the Reverend Ansel Bourne, whom James had treated himself and reported on in the *Principles*.

The Reverend Ansel Bourne of Greene, Rhode Island, had been a carpenter who, as a result of a temporary loss of sight and hearing, became converted from atheism to Christianity before he was thirty. From that time on he lived as an itinerant preacher, firm, self-reliant, and considered of upright character. On January 17, 1887, he withdrew a sum of money from the bank to pay for a parcel of land, got into a horse car, and then abruptly lost all memory of the events that followed. He did not return home, and when newspaper accounts listed him as missing, foul play was suspected.

On March 14, however, at Norristown, Pennsylvania, a man calling himself A. J. Brown, who had rented and stocked a small stationery store, filled it with confections, and carried on a quiet and unassuming trade, woke up in a fright and demanded of the people about him to tell him where he was. He declared he was the Reverend Ansel Bourne from Rhode Island and had no knowledge whatever of Norristown or the confection shop. All he remembered was drawing out money from the bank the day before. A Dr. Louis H. Read was called in, who thought him at first insane, until confirmatory reports were obtained from Providence, whereupon arrangements were made for Bourne to return home.

Bourne agreed in June 1890 to be hypnotized by James to see if in hypnotic trance his memory of "Brown" would come back. The experiment succeeded so well that he lost all memory of the Reverend Ansel Bourne, and all the facts of his normal life. While hypnotized, he did not recognize his wife, claiming never to have seen her before. On the other hand, he remembered all the details of his Norristown episode. The Brown personality, however, seemed nothing but a rather shrunken, dejected, and amnesiac extract of Mr. Bourne himself. To make the two personalities run into one continuous memory was James's intent, but no artifice would avail to accomplish this, and Mr. Bourne's skull, as James put it, continued to cover two distinct selves.[7]

James's notes continue with the facts surrounding the case

of Mollie Fancher, otherwise known at the time as the famous "Brooklyn enigma," another example of alternating personality that revealed not two but at least five distinct selves.[8]

Mollie Fancher was a healthy girl up to age fifteen, having survived the death of her mother and two siblings, the remarriage of her father, and the general vicissitudes of life under the care of her dead mother's sister, who also lived with the family. Then, in the spring of 1864, Mollie's health began to fail; she developed nervous indigestion, which led to anorexia, weakness, and fainting. Hysteria was suspected, and the doctors prescribed horseback riding, a common therapy of the day. But she met with a bad accident when thrown from a horse and suffered broken ribs, bleeding wounds, and unconsciousness.

During her recuperation Mollie suddenly developed partial blindness and double vision, but was eventually restored to a modicum of health. She soon became engaged to be married. Out shopping one day, she fell while alighting from a carriage, caught her dress as the horses pulled away, and was dragged some distance. When picked up, she was unconscious, again with broken bones. The marriage was canceled and she was put to bed, where she remained for the following fifty years.

After two years of progressive atrophy of the limbs, paralysis, and spasms, Mollie fell into a deep trance for one month, from which she revived, only to return to the paralysis again in periodic cycles. A nine-year period of nearly complete paralysis followed, in which she retained only limited movement. One arm was grotesquely contorted above her head; but her hands, both movable, were near each other. With great difficulty over the years she managed to produce bouquets of wax flowers, to do embroidery, and to write letters and keep a diary.

Sometime in 1875 she entered into a short unconscious state for a month, emerging with total amnesia for everything that had happened during the previous nine years.

Soon successive but separate personalities began to appear, calling themselves Sunbeam, Idol, Rosebud, Pearl, and Ruby. Each personality remembered a different segment of Mollie's life, and each manifested different qualities of her total personality. In addition, clairvoyant and extrasensory powers appeared at different times and were investigated in great detail by members of the press and certain medical authorities, all of whom Mollie eventually outlived. She began elaborate plans for a Fifty-Year Jubilee of her confinement in bed, but died on February 15, 1916, the day fixed for the celebration.

James's copy of *Mollie Fancher. "Who Am I?" An Enigma,* by A. H. Dailey, contains numerous penciled notations.[9] James was particularly interested in the emergence of the several alternate personalities, their traits, and their memories. He noted those investigators who were witness to these personalities and he cross-referenced their accounts with each other. He also noted Mollie's ability at mirror script and writing with her toes, and he cited instances of clairvoyant perception and the opening of what her biographer called her spiritual sight. Ostensibly, the reason why God put Mollie Fancher in this debilitated condition, Dailey had written, was to teach the world through her spiritual vision. But this assertion disregarded the fact that the multiple selves that appeared seemed, like Ansel Bourne, to be mere extracts of the total self.

James then introduces "Osgood Mason's case of Number One, Twooey, and The Boy." R. Osgood Mason was a New York doctor who had written an article on the phenomenon of duplex personality in the *Journal of Nervous and Mental Disease* in 1893, which James abstracted in the *Psychological Review* the following year:

"The case had been ten years under the observation of Dr. Mason, the primary personality being a young neurasthenic woman, thoughtful, dignified, and exhausted by much suffering. The second personality, which first supervened spontaneously after a syncope [or fugue] when she was twenty-four, was that of a sprightly child with a limited and quaint vocabulary, free from pain, able to take food, and fairly strong, named 'Twooey.' Its visits came at intervals through the years, and lasted from a few hours to a few days. During these years the patient, whose health had improved, got married. Later, 'Twooey' announced one day that she would never return, but that another visitor would take her place. Accordingly, after a syncope of several hours, a third personality, calling itself 'The Boy,' supervened, serious, and more like the primary self in character. The second and third selves had less acquired knowledge than the first one. Neither of the two former selves seems to be directly aware of both the preceding selves. They all know about each other by hearsay, however, and 'Twooey' and 'The Boy' have been very anxious to get 'Number One' well. 'The Boy' has sometimes lasted for weeks. 'Number One' seems to have had phenomena resembling clairvoyance; 'Twooey' to have shown sagacity amounting almost to prevision; 'The Boy' to have exhibited peculiar perceptive powers. . . ."[10]

With these interesting tidbits, James concludes that the case would seem to deserve a fuller account than the rather provocatively incomplete one the writer gives.

The notes refer next to Dr. Eugene Azam's widely known case of Felida X., also described briefly in the *Principles*: "At the age of fourteen this woman began to pass into a secondary state characterized by a change in her general disposition and character, as if certain inhibitions, previously existing, were suddenly removed. During the secondary state she remembered the first state, but on emerging from it into the first state she remembered nothing of the second. At the age of forty-four the duration of the second state (which was on the whole superior in quality to the original state) had gained upon the latter so much as to occupy most of her time. During it she remembers the events belonging to the original state, but her complete oblivion of the secondary state when the original state recurs is often very distressing to her, as for example, when the transition takes place in a carriage on her way to a funeral, and she hasn't the least idea which one of her friends might be dead. She actually becomes pregnant during one of her early secondary states, and in her first state had no knowledge of how it came to pass. Her distress at these blanks of memory is sometimes intense and once drove her to attempt suicide."[11]

James then introduces two cases described by Pierre Janet: first, that of "Mme. B.," otherwise known by the name of her other personality, "Léonie"; and second, the "Birth of Adrienne," an account of a secondary personality that emerged in the nineteen-year-old hysteric Lucie. Up to this time James has presented his audience with cases of alternating personality where multiple selves appear in succession. But these new examples by Janet point to several simultaneously operating personalities within the same person. Such discrete personalities, James had said in 1890, "are proved by M. Janet, not only to exist in successive forms in which we have seen them, but to *coexist*, to exist simultaneously." In other words, while the hysteric patient appears before the doctor helpless, floundering, all the time, "alive and kicking inside of the same person, other 'selves,' fully sensible and wide awake, proceed along, occupied with quite different concerns."

Janet had detailed the case of "Mme. B.," or "Léonie," in the *Revue philosophique* for 1886, and James had given a detailed account of it in his 1890 essay "The Hidden Self":

"This woman, whose life sounds more like an improbable romance than a genuine history, has had attacks of natural somnambulism since the age of three years. She has been hypnotized constantly, by all sorts of persons, from the age of sixteen upwards, and she is now forty-five. While her normal life developed in one way in the midst of her poor country surroundings, her second life was passed in drawing rooms and doctor's offices, and naturally took an entirely different direction. Today, when in her normal state, this poor peasant woman is a serious and rather sad person, calm and slow, very mild with everyone, and extremely timid; to look at her one would never suspect the personage which she contains. But hardly is she put to sleep hypnotically than a metamorphosis occurs. Her face is no longer the same. She keeps her eyes closed, it is true, but the acuteness of her other senses supplies their place. She is gay, noisy, restless, sometimes insupportably so. She remains good natured, but has acquired a singular tendency to irony and sharp jesting. Nothing is more curious than to hear her, after a sitting when she has received strangers who wished to see her asleep. She gives a word portrait of them, apes their manners, pretends to know their little ridiculous aspects and passions, and for each invents a romance. To this character must be added the possession of an enormous number of recollections, whose existence she does not even suspect when awake, for her amnesia is then complete. . . .

"She refuses the name of Léonie and takes that of Léontine (Léonie 2) to which her first magnetizers had accustomed her. 'That good woman is not myself,' she says, 'she is too stupid!' To herself, Léontine or Léonie 2, she attributes all the sensations and the actions, in a word all the conscious experiences which she has undergone in *somnambulism*, and knits them together to make the history of her already long life. To Léonie (as M. Janet calls the waking woman) on the other hand, she exclusively ascribes the events lived through in waking hours. [Janet says that he] was at first struck by an important exception to the rule, and was disposed to think that there might be something arbitrary in this partition of her recollections. In the normal state Léonie has a husband and children; but Léonie 2, the somnambulist, whilst acknowledging the children as her own, attributes the husband to The Other. This choice was perhaps explicable, but it followed no rule. It was not till later that [Janet] learned that her magnetizers in early days, as audacious as certain hypnotizers of recent date, had somnabulized her for her first accouchement [delivery], and that she had lapsed into that state spontaneously in the later ones. Léonie 2 was thus quite right in ascribing to herself the children—it was she who had had them, and the rule that her first trance state forms a different personality was not broken. But it is the same with her second and deepest state of trance. When after the renewed passes, syncope, etc., she reaches the condition which [Janet] called Léonie 3, she is another person still. Serious and grave, instead of being a restless child, she speaks slowly and moves but little. Again she separates herself from the waking Léonie 1. 'A good but rather stupid woman,' she says, 'and not me.' And she also separates herself from Léonie 2: 'How can you see anything of me in that crazy creature?' she says. 'Fortunately I am nothing for her.' "[12]

So far, then, James continues, "Janet's theory" is "plain sailing," that is, this splitting up of the mind into different parts is possible only where there is abnormal weakness, and consequently a defect of unifying or coordinating power. In the *Principles,* James had commented: "An hysterical woman abandons part of her consciousness because she is too weak nervously to hold it together. The abandoned part meanwhile may solidify into a secondary subconscious self. In a perfectly sound subject on the other hand, what is dropped out of mind at one moment keeps coming back at the next. The whole fund of knowledge and experience remains integrated, and no split off portion of it can get organized stably enough to form subordinate selves. When they do get so organized they naturally tend to take the form of a personality regardless of the size of the number of thoughts involved."[13]

James now goes on to discuss the "birth of Adrienne"—the moment in Janet's case of Lucie when her sub-personality came into being. Again, James had described the event in the *Principles*:

"In his anaesthetic somnambulist Lucie [Janet] found that when this young woman's attention was absorbed in conversation with a third party, her anaesthetic hand would write simple answers to questions whispered to her by himself. 'Do you hear?' he asked. 'No,' was the unconsciously written reply. 'But to answer you must hear.' 'Yes, quite so.' 'Then how do you manage?' 'I don't know.' 'There must be someone who hears these words I am speaking.' 'Yes.' 'Who?' 'Someone other than Lucie.' 'Ah! another person, shall we give her a name?' 'No.' 'Yes, it will be more convenient.' 'Well, Adrienne, then.' 'Once baptised, the subconscious personage,' M. Janet continues, 'grows more definitely outlined and displays better her psychological characters. In particular she shows us that she is conscious of the feelings excluded from the consciousness of the primary self. She it is who tells us that I am pinching the arm or touching the little finger in which Lucie for so long had no tactile sensations.' "[14]

There can be no doubt of the existence of a separate complex of organized thought that is dissociated from the primary waking state. Whether or not this is a true personality, however, is uncertain. Was it an organized complex merely waiting for a name? Or are the thoughts organized by the very act of naming? In which case the phenomenon of multiple selves is in some sense dependent on the sociocultural context in which it emerges, conditioned as much by the expectations of the experimenter as by the organization of the split-off fragment. Janet himself admits that, once named, the separate self develops more rapidly. Yet, while these are plausible explanations, the case of Adrienne does not rule out the possibility of independent personalities within the same person as a pre-existent phenomenon, nor does it rule out the invasion of personality by independent entities.

"Here we are at the great bifurcation of our interpretations," James tells his audience. "If we take one path," we keep to the rational, the acceptable, and the strictly scientific. "If the other we lead to psychical research. I said I would not enter there." He does, however, allude to the character of "Myers's theory."

In an article entitled "French Experiments on the Strata of Personality," Myers had examined Janet's case of Madame B. in light of the prevailing French theories. He then reiterated his own position, saying: "The arrangement with which we habitually identify ourselves—what we call the normal or primary self—consists, in my view, of elements selected for us in the struggle for existence with special reference to the maintenance of ordinary physical needs, and is not necessarily superior in any other respect to the latent personalities which lie alongside it—the fresh combinations of our elements which may be evoked, by accident or design, in a variety to which we can at present assign no limit."[15]

Myers considered that dreams, with so-called "mediumistic trance," as well as certain intoxications, epilepsies, hysterias, and recurrent insanities, afford examples of the development of what he called secondary mnemonic (memory) chains— fresh personalities, more or less complete, alongside the normal state.

Which brings us, says James now, to the topic of "mediumship." In the *Principles* he had written:

"In 'mediumships' or 'possessions' the invasion and the passing away of the secondary state are both relatively abrupt, and the duration of the state is usually short—from a few minutes to a few hours. Whenever the secondary state is well developed no memory for anything that happened during it remains after the primary consciousness comes back. The subject during the secondary consciousness speaks, writes or acts as if animated by a foreign person, and often names this foreign person, and gives his history. In old times the foreign 'control' was usually a demon, and is so now in communities which favor that belief. With us he gives himself out at the worst for an Indian or other grotesquely speaking but harmless personage. Usually he purports to be the spirit of a dead person known or unknown to those present, and the subject

is then what we call a 'medium.' Mediumistic possession in all
its grades seems to form a perfectly natural special type of
alternate personality, and the susceptibility to it in some form
is by no means an uncommon gift, in persons who have no
other obvious nervous anomaly."[16]

According to the prevailing view of the day, mediumship
was "produced by suggestion and imitation," says James,
citing "Cadwell and other developing circles." His notes refer
here to the work of J. W. Cadwell, mesmerist, whose
*"Delusion" of Spiritualism Compared with a Belief in the
Bible* James had in his library.[17] Cadwell specialized in mes-
merizing normal subjects; while they were entranced, he
would call forth a spirit control from the other world who
would speak through them. Cadwell traveled from state to
state holding what he called "developing circles," training
sessions to develop mediumistic powers. James may have been
referring to a specific instance of a developing circle that
Cadwell held in 1878 involving the return of his deceased
daughter, accompanied by the spirit of the still-living Frances
Morse, a lifelong friend and correspondent of James.[18] In any
event, Cadwell's instructions for becoming a medium were
fuel for the arguments of the orthodox medical community,
who viewed mediumship as nothing but the heightened
suggestibility of the subject patterned after a pathological
role model.

"This explanation fits many cases," James concludes,
especially when one considers the repetitious imitation seen in
"automatic writing," the most common form of mediumistic
communication. The anaesthetized hand might have a simple
letter suggested to it, an *n*, for instance, and the hand would
immediately begin reproducing *n* after *n* without effort. An *m*
or even a *p* might be suggested to it, and the hand would
begin to write the new letter, but in a moment it would
return to writing the *n*'s. Reflexive and automatic, this is the
lowest grade of automatic writing.

"But," James counters, "what of Mrs. Underwood's case?" —referring to the account of Mrs. Sarah Underwood given in the lecture on "Automatism." Spirit controls—distinctly different personalities from Mrs. Underwood's—had communicated the future outcome of events to her through automatic writing, events over which she had no control and of which she had no previous knowledge. And, he adds, "what shall we say to the case of Laurancy V.?" This is a reference to the Watseka Wonder, Laurancy Venuum, about whom James had written in the *Principles*. His intent was to suggest that these forms of mediumistic communication are highly sophisticated, and remain unaccounted for by the simple theory of suggestion and imitation:

"Laurancy was a young girl of fourteen, living with her parents at Watseka, Illinois, who, after various distressing hysterical disorders and spontaneous trances, during which she was possessed by departed spirits of a more or less grotesque sort, finally declared herself to be animated by the spirit of Mary Roff, a neighbor's daughter who had died in an insane asylum twelve years before, and insisted on being sent 'home' to Mr. Roff's house. After a week of 'homesickness' and importunity on her part her parents agreed, and the Roffs, who pitied her, and who were spiritualists into the bargain, took her in. Laurancy was said to be temporarily in heaven, and Mary's spirit now controlled her organism, and lived again in her former home.

"The new girl, now in her new home, seemed perfectly happy and content, knowing every person and everything that Mary knew when in her original body, twelve to twenty-five years ago, recognizing and calling by name those who were friends and neighbors of the family from 1852 to 1865, when Mary died, calling attention to scores, yes, hundreds of incidents that transpired during her natural life. During all the period of her sojourn at Mr. Roff's, she had no knowledge of, and did not recognize, any of Mr. Venuum's family, their friends or neighbors, yet Mr. and Mrs. Venuum and their children visited her and Mr. Roff's people, she being introduced to them as to any strangers. After frequent visits, and hearing them often and favorably spoken of, she learned to love them as aquaintances, and visited them with Mrs. Roff three times. From day to day she appeared natural, easy, affable, and industrious, attending diligently and faithfully to her household duties, assisting in the general work of the family as a faithful, prudent daughter might be supposed to do, singing, reading, or conversing as opportunity offered, upon all matters of private or general interest to the family.

"The so-called Mary, whilst at the Roffs', would sometimes 'go back to heaven,' and leave the body in a 'quiet trance,' i.e., without the original personality of Laurancy returning. After eight or nine weeks, the memory and manner of Laurancy would sometimes partially, but not entirely, return for a few minutes.

"Once Laurancy seems to have taken possession for a short time. At last, after some fourteen weeks, conformably to the prophecy which 'Mary' had made when she first assumed 'control,' she departed definitely and the Laurancy-consciousness came back for good. Mr. Roff writes that Laurancy asked to be taken to the Venuum home. Treating him now as an acquaintance, she greeted her real family with loving affection. She said that things seemed like a dream to her, but that she acted, according to reports, perfectly natural and seemed well. Laurancy's mother wrote some months later that she still seemed natural, although she felt as if what she had been before her sickness was still like a dream. She has been smarter, more intelligent, more industrious, and more polite and womanly than ever before. The Venuum family was most grateful to the Roffs for helping to effect a cure of their daughter through spiritualist means; otherwise Laurancy surely would have died, or been permanently confined to an insane asylum, and perhaps died there. Eight years later, Laurancy was reported to be married and a mother in good health. She had apparently outgrown the mediumistic phase of her existence."[19]

"The truth is," James acknowledges to his audience, "that we see here the complexity of Nature." Janet's formula, that these are merely split-off fragments of the primary personality, is "not descriptive" of such cases as these just mentioned. "Myers's is better."[20] Myers's notion fits both the cases described by Janet as pathological, and also the more exceptional instances that suggest the possibility of a transcendent dimension in the spectrum of subconscious states—the presence just below the threshold of a domain far wiser than and superior to that of normal, waking, rational awareness.

"I am at the portal of Psychical Research onto which I said I would not enter," James says again, hesitating.[21] "But I suppose that it would be overcautious in me, and disappoint some of my hearers if I did not say here frankly what I think of the relation of the cases I have dwelt on to these supernormal cases. I put forth my impression merely as such and with great diffidence. The only thing I am absolutely sure of being the extreme complication of the facts.

"Some minds would see a marvel in the simplest hypnosis—others would refuse to admit that there was anything new even if one rose from the dead. They would either deny the apparition or say you could find a full explanation of it in Foster's *Physiology*. Of these minds, one pursues the idols of the tribe, another of the cave. Both may be right in respect to a portion of the facts. I myself have no question that the formulae of dissociated personality will account for the phenomena I have brought before you. . . . Hypnotism is sleep, hysteria is obsession, Janet's phrase suffices here; 'Not by demons, but by a fixed idea of the person that has dropt down.'

"But to say that is one thing and to *deny all other meanings* of the phenomena is another. Whether supernormal powers of cognition in certain persons may occur is a matter to be decided by evidence. If they can occur, it may be that there must be a 'chink' [or opening in the filtering mechanism that separates consciousness from the subconscious—a loosening of the bonds, so to speak, that so tightly restrict the expansion of consciousness beyond its normal boundaries].

"The hypnotic condition is not in and of itself clairvoyant, but it is more *favorable* to the cause of clairvoyance or thought transference than the waking state," James concludes. "So likewise with experiences of alternate personality. The tendency for the self to break up may, if there be spirit influences, yield them their opportunity. Thus we might have hysteric mediums; and if there were real demons they might possess only hysterics. Thus each side may see a portion of the truth. I believe that Hodgson, Myers, and Sedgwick in obstinately refusing to start with any theories, in patiently accumulating facts, are following in the footsteps of the great scientific tradition of Moseley.[22] I myself am convinced of supernormal cognition and supernormal healing. The facts are there . . . but as yet I have not a vestige of a theory."[23]

"So now I return to our lectures!" Once again the notes suggest that James had not originally intended to enter into such subjects. He concludes with an announcement of the next lecture subject, "Demon Possession."

: LECTURE V :
DEMONIACAL
POSSESSION

———

"Our knowledge of altered personality has made rapid strides in recent years," James opens this fifth lecture, "showing us numerous mutations in our present sense of self."[1] He then names the three principal types: "insane, hysteric, and somnambulistic," recapitulating the previous lecture. "We saw the transient altered personality of epileptic insanity, and certain dream states described under the name of 'ambulatory automatism'—the subject going from home and returning after an interval of perhaps weeks, with the memory of what had happened during his wandering utterly effaced." And he refers again to the case of Ansel Bourne, whom James himself had treated by using hypnotic suggestion to bring back the memory of the lost interval.[2]

"But there is a fourth type," he reminds the audience, "that of 'spirit control' or mediumship." Citing Robert Charles Caldwell's work, "where mediumship in the past has been equated with devil worship and pathology,"[3] James implies that by his own era, "no one now regards it as insanity. [It is] different from the insane delusions of altered personality.

"History shows that mediumship is identical with demon possession," he comments. "But the obsolescence of public

93

belief in the possession by demons is a very strange thing in Christian lands, when one considers that it is the one most articulately expressed doctrine of both Testaments, and . . . reigned for seventeen hundred years, hardly challenged, in all the churches. Every land and every age has exhibited the facts on which this belief was founded. India, China, Egypt, Africa, Polynesia, Greece, Rome, and all medieval Europe believed that certain nervous disorders were of supernatural origin, inspired by gods and sacred; or by demons"—and therefore diabolical. "When the pagan gods became demons, all possession became diabolic, and we have the medieval condition." James then cites Montaigne. Michel de Montaigne, the sixteenth-century French essayist and philosopher, had called for an admission of ignorance by the persecutors of witches because they had no real proof of the charges against the accused; he also called for moderation in their fanaticism at extracting confessions.

Referring to the spiritualistic activities of Boston and New York in 1896, James states that the diabolic nature of demon possession now "has with us assumed a benign and optimistic form, [in which] changed personality is considered the spirit of a departed being coming to bring messages of comfort from the 'sunny land.' "[4]

This more optimistic mediumship, says James, "differs from all the classic types of insanity. Its attacks are periodic and brief, usually not lasting more than an hour or two, and the patient is entirely well between them, and retains no memory of them when they are over. During them, he speaks in an altered voice and manner, names himself differently, and describes his natural self in the third person as he would a stranger. The new impersonation offers every variety of completeness and energy, from the rudimentary form of unintelligible automatic scribbling, to the strongest convulsions with blasphemous outcries, or the most fluent inspirational speech."

Next, James launches into a remarkable series of examples of alleged demon possession from different Eastern cultures, citing accounts from Japan, China, and southern India. Each instance shows characteristics of the subliminal that he had outlined in his first four lectures, but now the subliminal is seen at work in the social sphere.

He begins with reports of miracles in Samoa, then turns to the work of Mr. Percival Lowell, who said that in Japan, particularly among the Ryobu Shinto sect of Buddhism, there were a number of priests who associated themselves with the spirit of a particular mountain god by cultivating the power of passing into trances. Lowell, astronomer and world traveler, was a member of the Lowell family of Boston and well known to James.[5]

James's lecture notes here show only "Ontaké, Percival Lowell, p. 153." But James's copy of Lowell's *Occult Japan* contains numerous marginal marks, and on page 153 is the notation "read"—meaning either read carefully or read this example to the audience. The account in question concerned an ascent of Mount Ontaké that Lowell made with a companion. Having taken an irregular route used only by priests, Lowell and his friend were able to witness numerous trance rites performed by priests who would stop at designated intervals in the climb to the summit. The setting James describes to his audience was the ceremonial ground of a ritual hut near the top of the mountain.

Lowell gave details of the ceremony. The priest, surrounded by his followers, after a little private finger-twisting and prayer, folded his hands and closed his eyes while the others began chanting. One of them took a wand and placed it in the priest's hands. The priest at once fell slowly forward on it, resting one end on the mat and the other against his forehead. His followers took up in chorus a stirring processional chant. As the measured cadence rolled on, suddenly the wand began to quiver and the chant increased in energy.

Moment by moment the wand gathered motion by fits and lulls, as when a storm gathers in a clear sky. The paroxysm came on, and then the wand settled with a jerk, a suppressed quiver alone still thrilling through it. The god had come.

One of the onlookers came forward and addressed the outstretched wand, reverently asking the god's name. The eyes of the possessed had already opened to the glassy stare typical of trances, the eyeballs so rolled back that the pupils were nearly out of sight. In an unnatural, yet not exactly artificial voice, the god replied, "Matsuwo," at which the questioner bowed again, turned to Lowell, and asked if he had any questions to ask the spirit now present. He asked only about the health of his family back in Boston and the outcome of an approaching voyage. All his questions were answered with delphic oracularity, after which the god spoke of his own accord. The god spoke *to* the questioner, but *at* Lowell. He thanked Lowell for climbing Mount Ontaké successfully two years before. Lowell was pleased, considering that the pious natives were convinced no foreigner could scale the sacred peak and return alive.

Immediately after this, the possessed priest settled forward into a lethargic swoon. From it he was roused by further incantation into fresh fury. Slowly raising the wand, he suddenly beat the air above his head, and proceeded to hop excitedly around on his folded legs, stopping at each of the four compass points to repeat his performance. Then he came back to his previous commanding pose, and, in reply to a question, spoke again. Once more he lapsed into lethargy, and once more he was roused and answered. When he had fallen into his comatose condition for the third time, the questioner came up and made a benediction by signing a Sanskrit character on his back and slapped him energetically on top of it. One of the four aides stood by with a cup of water, and the moment he had sufficiently revived, put it to his lips and helped him to drink. Under this treatment he gradually recovered, but it took some kneading before the wand could be loosened from his cataleptic grip.[6]

James next tells his audience of instances known in China and Japan of possession by foxes; and his notes refer to "Nevius, p. 104, *Foxes.*"

The Reverend John Nevius was a missionary stationed at Ningpo, in eastern China, under the Reverend H. V. Rankin. While trying to convert the local Chinese to Christianity, Nevius had observed the high prevalance of demon possession among the people. Knowing little about the practices of popular Taoism, he was struck with the idea that certain passages in the New Testament might be used both to effect a cure and to win new converts. Amazed at his subsequent success, Nevius sent circulars to missions throughout China inquiring about any wider prevalence of the phenomenon of possession. Collating the reported instances with his own cases, he added an overview of similar cases throughout the Orient which he gleaned from popular literature, then produced a large manuscript, *Demon Possession and Allied Themes.*[7]

In James's copy of the work, page 104 carries his characteristic marginal markings next to Nevius's discussion of possession by foxes in Japan. According to Nevius, Chinese notions concerning the superhuman power of the fox entered Japan in the Middle Ages, and the belief spread until every person had a circumstantial fox tale to relate. Nevius described the belief that the fox entered the afflicted person through the breast or in the space between the fingernails and the flesh. It took up its abode inside, and lived a life completely separate from the proper self of the host. The person possessed hears and understands everything that the fox inside says or thinks, and the two often engage in loud and violent dispute, while the fox speaks in an unnatural voice to the person.

The only difference between cases of possession in the Bible and those that pertain to foxes in Japan, Nevius stressed, was that in Japan the possessed were all women of the lower class, of weak intellect, with a superstitious turn of mind or afflicted with some debilitating disease. Possession never occurred except in subjects who had suffered it already or who believed in the reality of its existence.

James read out to his audience one such case, reported from the hospital at the Imperial University of Japan. The attending physician was called in to treat a girl with typhoid fever, who later recovered. While the girl was on the ward, she overheard a conversation between two women. One thought she was possessed by a fox and wished to pass it on to someone else in order to be rid of it. At that moment the girl experienced an extraordinary sensation: the fox had taken possession of her. All efforts to rid herself of him were in vain. She would cry out each time she felt him take possession of her thoughts, and in a strange, cracked, dry voice the fox would speak and mock his unfortunate host.

This continued for three weeks, until a Buddhist priest from the Nichiren sect was called for. The priest upbraided the fox for his behavior, and the fox, always speaking through the girl's mouth, argued the other side. Finally the fox declared he was tired of the girl and demanded certain gifts to be placed on a certain altar at a specific time on a certain day in exchange for leaving her. All the while the girl was conscious of the words her lips were made to frame but was powerless to say anything in her own person. On the appointed day the offering was given, and the fox quit the girl at the very hour prescribed.[8]

In India, instances of this kind of possession were extremely common, James continues. He then cites an example from the work of R. C. Caldwell, who had written a somewhat demeaning and overinflated literary account of a possession rite in southern India for the *Contemporary Review* (1876). Nevertheless, James thought Caldwell's description useful. James's notes give a page reference for Caldwell's article, which was entitled "Demonolatry, Devil-Dancing, and Demoniacal

Possession," and James's copy of the journal (the complete set of which was given to Widener Library at Harvard after he died) contains his extensive marginal markings. In the article Caldwell described a certain banyan tree, under which regular offerings of brandy and cheroots were made by the natives in order to propitiate the spirit of a white man who had died at its base. A plague had beset the land and the natives suspected that the dead man's spirit was responsible. Thus a priest was called in to perform the necessary sacrifice and quell the plague.

Emphasizing the drama of the performance, Caldwell described the devil priest, sacrificial knife in hand, reeling into the middle of an assembled crowd who had brought offerings. Of these people he remained utterly and completely unconscious. While he was chanting and swaying, his fingers soon began to twitch and his head wagged in an "unnatural fashion." The convulsions increased with the beat of the tom-toms, and he began to sweat profusely:

"Suddenly there is a yell, a stinging, stunning cry, an ear-piercing shriek, a hideous abominable gobble-gobble of hellish laughter, and the devil dancer had sprung to his feet, eyes protruding, mouth foaming, chest heaving, muscles quivering, and outstretched arms swollen and straining as if they were crucified!"

The priest began to cry out that he was God, and the assembly crowded around to offer their gifts and solicit answers to their questions, "Shall I die of cholera this time?" "Bless my sick child and heal it." The shrieks, vows, incantations, prayers, and exclamations of thankful praise rose up from the crowd to a frenzied pitch, goaded on by the stentorian howls and ghoulish laughter of the priest, who by this time was jumping up and down hacking and hewing at himself with his knife.

His answers to the queries put to him were generally incoherent. Sometimes he was sullenly silent, and sometimes, while the blood from his self-inflicted wounds mingled freely with that of the sacrifice, he was most benign, showering his divine favors of health and prosperity all around him. Hours passed by. The trembling crowd stood rooted to the spot. Suddenly the dancer gave a great bound in the air; when he descended, he was motionless. The fiendish look had vanished from his eyes. His demoniacal laughter was stilled. He spoke to this and that neighbor quietly and reasonably. He laid aside his garb, washed his face at the nearest rivulet, and walked soberly home, a modest, well-conducted man."[9]

James follows this with another example: the first case of possession ever treated in China by John Nevius, the "case of Kwo." A page number in Nevius's *Demon Possession and Allied Themes* is quoted in the lecture notes corresponding to where James has marked a long account in the book. But James had also summarized the case in his critique of Nevius for the *Psychological Review* (1895):

"Kwo . . . having bought a picture of the goddess Wang, had been visited by a demon-counterfeit of the goddess in a dream who told him she had taken up her abode in his house. Various neurotic conditions and disorderly impulses had followed, ending in an attack of frenzy during which, the man being unconscious, the demon spoke through his lips, demanding incense, worship, etc. As usual, the demands were met by the family, and the demon thereafter made periodical visitations, throwing the man into unconsciousness and speaking through his organism, healing the diseases of visitors, and giving practical advice. On Dr. Nevius assuring Kwo that conversion to Christianity would rid him of encumbrance, he became baptized, the trance state only recurring once afterwards, and the dream bidding a formal farewell on that occasion. Fourteen years have passed without relapse. Kwo has had persecutions and trials but no return of his malady, and neither he nor his neighbors think of doubting that he was rescued from the dominion of an evil spirit through faith and trust in Christ."[10]

"One sees that the type [of demonic possession] is modified by the traditions of the country," comments James. And he now goes on to cite a number of similar examples in the history of European civilization.

Although historically the witchcraft delusion had been explained in various ways, to James witches were not neuropathic persons; but their accusers were. He had examined the witchcraft trials carefully, and had found that they invariably started with some "demon disease" in the neighborhood. These demon diseases, which were common in those days, could arise from many different functional or traumatically induced neuropathic diseases. If there were no obvious physical disorders, and the symptoms did not yield readily to the usual medical treatment, the case was considered to be one of demoniacal possession.[11]

James's notes then cite "Boguet p. 1," which refers to the *Discours des sorciers* (*Examination of Witches*), written in 1603 by Henri Boguet, chief justice in the district of Saint-Claude in Burgundy. The case that James chose to read to his audience involved a young girl called Loyse Maillat:

"On Saturday the fifth of June in the year 1598 Loyse the eight-year-old daughter of Claude Maillat was struck helpless in all limbs so that she had to go on all-fours; also she kept twisting her mouth about in a very strange manner. She continued thus afflicted for a number of days, until on the 19th of July her father and mother, judging from her appearance that she was possessed, took her to the Church of Our Saviour to be exorcised. There were then found five devils, whose names were Wolf, Cat, Dog, Jolly and Griffon; and when the priest asked the girl who had cast the spell on her, she answered that it was Françoise Secretain, whom she pointed out from among all those who were present at her exorcism. But as for that day, the devils did not go out of her.

"But when the girl had been taken back to her parents' house, she begged them to pray to God for her, assuring them

that if they fell to their prayers she would quickly be delivered. Accordingly they did so at the approach of night, and
as soon as her father and mother had done praying the girl
told them that two of the devils were dead, and that if they
persevered with their devotions they would kill the remaining
ones also. Her father and mother were anxious for their
daughter's health and did not cease praying all night. The
next morning at dawn the girl was worse than usual and kept
foaming at the mouth; but at last she was thrown to the
ground and the devils came out of her mouth in the shape
of balls as big as the fist and red as fire, except the Cat, which
was black. The two which the girl thought to be dead came
out last and with less violence than the three others; for they
had given up the struggle from the first, and for this reason
the girl had thought they were dead. When all these devils
had come out, they danced three or four times round the fire
and then vanished; and from that time the girl began to
recover her health."[12]

James remarks that these descriptions remind one of the
classical hysterical attacks—the lump in the throat, known as
"globus hystericus," the convulsive seizures, and so forth.
They appear to be examples of neuropathic imitative hysteria,
meaning outbreaks patterned after other cases prevalent at that
time, which highly susceptible individuals then mimicked.

Next, James presents a similar example that could be found
in cases of "imitative chorea" (St. Vitus' dance), but he gives
no details except to note "Mitchell '69," probably meaning
work by the Philadelphia neurologist Silas Weir Mitchell,
who had written up the Mary Reynolds case. Chorea is a
neurological disorder identified by exaggeration of voluntary
movements that are purposeless and that occur simultaneously;
"imitative chorea" was the name given to the spread of chorea
by mimicry.[13] The case reported by James probably refers to
Mitchell's article in an 1869 issue of *The American Journal
of Medical Sciences*. There Mitchell described examples of
imitative chorea among soldiers wounded in the Civil War,

men who showed the neurologic signs of chorea but were actually recovering from gunshot wounds. He had observed that these signs were still in evidence long after the healing of the tissues and nerves had taken place.[14]

James seems to imply here that there is an important similarity between the imitative hysteria in cases of wholesale possession and Mitchell's observations of the traumatic effect of shock to the nerves in these soldiers. He then tells his audience: "these cases suggest that differences in the different countries came from differences in the particular psychological climate, but the general features are the same."*

"Many interesting reports had been published in later years of chorea epidemics, supposed to have resulted from imitation," James continues. "These epidemics had been known to last for months or even years." One interesting case of demoniacal possession had been reported in France by Dr. Augustin Constans in Savoy, in the town of Morzine, during 1863. James also noted a similar epidemic that had been reported in Italy by Giuseppe Chiap and Fernando Franzolini.

The epidemic of Morzine had started in the late 1850s when a young girl, on her way to a religious service, had witnessed the drowning death of another girl.[15] Several days later she developed convulsive seizures, which were subsequently attributed to the devil. Eventually, her sisters became

* As a result of newspaper clippings sent to him from Atlanta by a former student and colleague, the famous social scientist and reformer W. E. B. DuBois, in 1903, James published a strongly worded caution against the lynching of Negroes in the South, which at that time had reached epidemic proportions. He called for immediate heroic remedies against this profound social disease, which he said was in danger of becoming an established custom on the verge of institutionalization. Certain rabid individuals were to blame, and the rest were mere followers whose passions had been momentarily inflamed. The result was a fusion of fierce animal appetites with perverted ideal emotions that completely swept normally civilized people off their feet. See James's "A Strong Note of Warning Regarding the Lynching Epidemic"— *Springfield Daily Republican,* July 23, 1903, p. 11.

similarly infected. Within a few months, more children were affected. Each separate symptom that a victim displayed was ascribed to a different devil. First children, then older people became possessed. All the cases of possession were attributed to a look or a touch purportedly given by a certain person. Two of those most frequently accused were an old woman named Chauplanez, and a young man, Jean Berger, who was an assistant to the town mayor. By 1858, only twenty-seven people had shown the symptoms, seventeen of whom were cured by religious exorcism, and one upon the threat of murder by her father.

But one of the attempted exorcisms was such a failure that it produced a flood of possessed persons and the total number affected could not be counted. By 1860 there were 110 clearly recognized cases.

Then a hypnotizer came into the village and announced that he would cure everyone. After his usual techniques failed to work, he resorted to more dramatic ministrations, only making matters worse. Eventually the townspeople became an uncontrollable mob. On one occasion, they marched to a nearby chapel with clubs and torches looking for the retired vicar, on the assumption that he had had a hand in starting the possessions. They sacrificed a goat at the chapel, hoping to lay a curse on the vicar so he would die in eighteen days from that time and his spell would be ended. On the day he was supposed to have died, a woman imagined that the spirit of the vicar entered into her stomach and gave her convulsions, even though the vicar was, in fact, still alive.

Jean Berger was also one of the victims of the villagers' attacks. Eight days before Dr. Constans had arrived, Berger was chased by a group of thirty or forty persons who thought him responsible for possessing the townspeople. Men, women, and children, sick and well, armed with rocks, axes, and sticks, pursued him for more than three hours, but he managed to escape. His reputation for helping as a local public servant should have saved him, but it evidently made things worse. Good, honest citizens who showed Dr. Constans around told him that Berger and one or two others "would have to have their throats cut" in order for the epidemic to end.

Constans gave details of the various symptoms of the convulsive crises. He pointed out that these agreed with similar conditions described by Charcot—shaking, tremor, fright, agitated movements of the eyes, convulsions over major areas of the body, and emotional outbursts of anger and excitement alternating very rapidly with depression. Victims when directly addressed would always relate their answer to some fixed idea. Usually passive among themselves, they became offensive to strangers and used insulting words that they ascribed to the devils. They burst into dramatic displays of anger in which they would hurl furniture or fall to the floor, roll over, and bound up all in one movement, and so on. In time the crisis would subside. They would then stand up, brush themselves off, and resume their previous activities as if nothing had happened. Constans noted a complete absence of erotic behavior or removal of clothes. In fact, many of the stricken women would convulse in such a way as to protect their dresses from improperly exposing their undergarments.

As for the cure, Constans stressed a moral approach. Members of the clergy who knew nothing of the town's history were brought in to replace those in office. An army brigade was sent into the area and its arrival produced the expected feeling of intimidation among the townspeople, and the conviction that the authorities were determined to end the epidemic. Since the crisis had often happened in church during Mass, Constans arranged with the army to have anyone carried away who caused a disturbance during the service. The success of these measures proved to Constans that the power of will and observing self-control regulated the appearance and disappearance of the crisis. The effect, however, was one of postponement rather than termination.

His most effective measure was the separation of the towns-people from each other, as their collective impressions had the effect of provoking the same excitement in still others and seemed to heighten the ease with which the crisis was initiated. All affected persons were sent away to different places to live and the epidemic finally ended. This was thought to be a more humane measure than the confinement of certain individuals, or simply quarantining certain segments of the population.[16]

James's notes also cite "Chiap e Franzolini . . . Verzegniss" —a reference to the work of Giuseppe Chiap and Fernando Franzolini, two Italian doctors who reported on the outbreak of an epidemic of hystero-demonopathy in the Italian town now known as Monte Verzegnis in 1878.[17]

The mental epidemic began with a single hysteric subject, who was thought by the townspeople to be possessed once it was reported that she had gone through a severe convulsive crisis. Simple hysteria was common enough among certain young women in each village; but the combination of a single severe case and local gossip, entrenched as it was in deep-seated superstitions, fanned the delusion into a widespread epidemic. Unusual rituals and sermons took place at the church, confessions increased, neighboring villagers came to investigate, and more cases appeared, until forty parishioners were afflicted. Exorcism by the church became a regular occurrence in the village homes, which only made matters worse. Most of the victims of the demon disease were particularly susceptible to religious objects, the sound of the church bell ringing, the sight of a priest, and so on.

The symptoms included minor characteristics of digestive troubles, hyperaesthesia, anaesthetic areas, and during the major crisis, contractions, paralysis, unconsciousness, delirium, swearing, aversion to anything religious, and the alleged invasion by independent personalities who claimed clairvoyant powers and identified themselves as demons recently departed from dead persons in other villages.

Chiap and Franzolini compared the possession of persons at Verzegniss in detail with the epidemic in Morzine described by Constans. Relying heavily on Charcot's interpretation that much of what was witnessed arose from functional nervous disorders having neither physical nor supernatural origin, the Italian doctors prescribed a cure that paralleled Constans's closely. The two most severe cases were confined in a hospital; others were sent to nearby villages. All exorcisms were banned. The church bell no longer rang at night. Priests were instructed to cease the performance of special services. All publicity about the event was suppressed. As a result, the epidemic subsided, although the doctors admitted that it was not eradicated, but only confined now within families.

James notes that, in addition to the combination of a single hysterical case and local superstition, the problem was probably compounded by a high incidence of inbreeding among the local population, which created a tendency toward increased nervous troubles. Otherwise the population was in fine, robust health. The doctors were particularly interested in the fate of the two worst cases, Margherita and Lucia. Margherita was the original hysteric subject from whom all the others were infected. She had been mildly hysteric most of her life, and it was only after her first major crisis that, as the local population talked of possession, she began to manifest the obliging signs. Lucia was less affected; and when removed to the hospital for some months, she became completely well. After she returned to her home environment, however, the crises reappeared. As for Margherita, her case was deemed incurable.[18]

James then reports a modern instance of possession that occurred in Bavaria. His notes cite the case of Michael Zilk, described by the monks of Wemding, and written up in a French publication, *Le Diable au XIXe siècle*, by one Dr. Bataille.[19] Michael Zilk, a ten-year-old boy and son of a mill-owner, suddenly developed a violent reaction to prayer. He could not pray or hear anyone else pray without falling into an extraordinary fury. He could not bear to have near him any religious object. This developed into the performance of extremely gross displays before his parents, during which his face and mannerisms became completely transformed. A medical doctor was called in but without result. The parents turned to the clergy, who said it was a case of demon possession, and an exorcism was called for. After wading through much ecclesiastical red tape, they received the proper permissions, and the exorcism was performed by the monks of Wemding. The ritual was described in detail in Bataille's book.*

"Hystero-demonopathy is the name given to these symptoms," James comments, "a suggestive disease; and no one could fail to recognize in these attacks the analogy to the performance of the numerous spiritualistic mediums of our present time." This is the main point of James's lecture—that the demon possession of old has now been transformed into an optimistic mediumship, related not to devil worship

---

* Unknown to James, this was a completely fictitious account, invented by a cohort of anti-clerical writers in France and Italy led by Gabriel Jogand-Pages, alias Dr. Leo Taxil, and another man known only as Dr. Bataille. Taxil had begun as a virulent critic of the Church, only to recant his sins and ostensibly launch an extensive exposé of French Freemasonry as a church representative. The fiendish imagination of Taxil, Bataille, and their friends stopped at nothing in their invention of lurid pornographic scenes of Freemason rites that were designed to be particularly repugnant to their supposedly very pious and moral, but really very avid, readers. Taxil's purpose was to expose what he felt was the hypocrisy of the institutional Church by inventing his accounts of the Freemasons. However, the hoax went unexposed until the end of the 1890s, when Taxil's charades had gone too far, and people started to suspect he was a fraud. He arranged a dramatic dénounement, hinting that he would admit the truth, but then mysteriously dropped from sight. The Catholic press, the clergy, and a large popular readership on both sides of the Atlantic had been taken in, mostly by their own gullibility, combined with the advantage Taxil took of the power the Church exerted over the lives of the common people.

and psychopathology but to personal growth, healing, especially of functional disorders, and to religious or philosophical concerns. There had been a distinct, though gradual, change from a damaging character to the recent comparatively beneficent character of such phenomena. James's own view was that it was a law of the secondary consciousness that mediumship should take the religious form, although he had no explanation to offer as to why this was so.

On February 1, 1879, James was to write to Henry William Rankin from Newport, Rhode Island, expanding these same ideas:

"One of my lectures in New York is at the Academy of Medicine before the Neurological Society, the subject being 'Demoniacal Possession.' I shall, of course, duly advertise the Nevius book. I am not as positive as you are . . . in the belief that the obsessing agency is really demonic individuals. I am perfectly willing to adopt that theory if the facts lend themselves best to it, for who can trace limits to the hierarchies of personal existence in the world? But the lower stages of automatism shade off so continuously into the highest supernormal manifestations, through the intermediary ones of imitative hysteria and 'suggestibility,' that I feel as if no one *general* theory as yet would cover all the facts. So that the most I will plead for before the neurologists is the recognition of demon possession as a regular 'morbid-entity' whose commonest homologue is the 'spirit-control' observed in test mediumship, and which tends to become the more benign and less alarming, the less pessimistically it is regarded. This last remark seems certainly to be true. Of course I will ignore the sporadic cases of old fashioned malignant possession which still occur today. I am convinced that we stand with all these things at the threshold of a long enquiry, of which the end appears as yet to no one, least of all myself. And I believe that the best theoretic work yet done in the subject is the beginning made by F. W. H. Myers in his papers in the *Proceedings of the English Society for Psychical Research.*

The first thing is to start the medical profession out of its idiotically *conceited ignorance* of all such matters—matters which have everywhere and at all times played a vital part in human history."[20]

And so, James now addresses his audience, "It would be strange indeed, if a phenomenon which had played such a large part in history should have died out without leaving anything in its place. Medical men should learn from all this a certain lesson, i.e., that as our views had become optimistic, instead of pessimistic, the whole thing had become harmless. We live in a day when there is much alarmist writing in psychopathy about degeneration, and the alarming significance of all sorts of symptoms and signs, so that there is danger of drawing the line of health too narrowly."

But "if there are devils," he concludes, "if there are supernormal powers, it is through the cracked and fragmented self that they enter. We see this chink [or direct exposure of the highly suggestible, secondary subwaking self] in the medieval accusations"; and thus, we have our "transition to witchcraft" —the subject of James's next lecture.

Some of the comments of members of the New York Neurological Society who heard James redeliver his lecture on "Demoniacal Possession" at the New York Academy of Medicine on February 2, 1879, are germane here.

Dr. C. A. Herter said that the idea of connecting the powers of modern spiritualistic mediums with the peculiar forms of demoniacal possession that occurred in former years was a most interesting one. This fact had been brought out most interestingly and impressively in the address. He had been much interested in the gradual change from the damaging to the comparatively beneficent aspect of these phenomena.

A Mr. Martin said that it seemed to him rather remarkable that the suggestions which occurred to the possessed person related almost entirely to ethical matters or religious subjects. A large portion of the recorded cases he had met with referred to the possession by devils, who were leading the person astray or into immortality. He would like to ask whether Professor James had observed the same thing.

James replied that it was a law of the secondary consciousness that it took the religious form. He had no explanation to offer, however, of this law. It was a singular fact that involuntary writing was apt to take the spiritualistic forms. This would occur in the case of persons who had no intellectual hospitality for that view, and who had not been exposed to spiritualistic influences. Spirits, religious truths, and philosophical discourses were the style of these communications.

Dr. Mary Putnam Jacobi said that, as in so many cases of melancholia, the grief was about having sinned against the Holy Ghost, even in persons who had had no religious or Calvinistic instruction. She would like to ask whether Professor James considered it an example of the phenomena just spoken of. She would also like to ask his opinion of an essay that had been published by Barrett Wendell of Harvard, entitled "Were the Salem Witches Entirely Guiltless?" According to this essay, although these witches were not possessed by devils, they were abandoning themselves to impulses coming from the lower structures of their natures—the result of ancestral influences.

James replied that he did not think the delusions of melancholia had anything to do with the subject under discussion. The sin against the Holy Ghost was only an endeavor to explain the grief that was felt. Regarding the essay by Professor Wendell, he would say that at the time of the witchcraft belief, there were certainly persons attempting to do what they could by diabolical aid, but in all probability they formed a very small part of it. In Salem, the girls from whom the accusations emanated had been having hypnotic séances with a West Indian slave, who was herself practically insane. They passed then into such a condition that they were accused of witchcraft, and were tried under such circumstances as to impress them powerfully by suggestion. From what we know of imitative hysteria, the whole matter was entirely explicable on that basis, without any supposition of guilt upon the part of these children. It was a suggestive epidemic of a semi-hysterical nervous disorder.

Dr. Charles Loomis Dana then said that the speaker had made quite clear the relation of trance to demoniacal possession of old, but he would like to know how widespread this condition was now. He knew that about fifteen years ago spiritualism had been immensely prevalent in the eastern states. If the condition had continued to exist and spread, there was certainly much more in the United States today than in civilized countries several hundred years ago.

James replied that it would be difficult to answer this question statistically, as he had no trustworthy statistics. We do know, however, that at the present time there are many "faith-healers."[21]

:LECTURE VI:
WITCHCRAFT

James opens his sixth lecture by recounting for his audience recent accusations of witchcraft and possession from Bavaria, France, and even from Cape Cod. His notes indicate that in the nineteenth century there were still reports of a large number of cases of witch slaying in all parts of Europe. "At San Jacopo in Mexico five witches were burnt together in 1877 by legal process. This very year in Ireland," cases were also reported.[1] "So witchcraft is not extinct then."

"At all times there has been belief in sorcerers and evil spirits," he comments in the notes. "But the witch period proper is that of belief in a compact with Satan, 1250–1650, while the proper devil's period was 1475 to 1600. This was a time of intellectual flowering in its highest bloom—the revival of learning, the birth of modern thought, the Protestant reformation, and the discovery of the New World. It was a time of the Renaissance in Italy, where culture expanded in all directions, especially in the arts. It was the time of Copernicus, Shakespeare, Bacon, Vesalius, Kepler, Galileo, and Descartes." Yet in the midst of this age, adds James, there was widespread belief in witchcraft.

The period of the Middle Ages was in fact a time when vast mental epidemics swept over Europe. Often instigated by a handful of individuals, such epidemics would spread until entire nations convulsed in hysterical insanity. The Crusades were the first great European example of mass hysteria. They began when just a few, then thousands, were irresistibly drawn to visit the Holy Land. This led to the inevitable conflict with the Middle Eastern culture. The Turks took Palestine, and Europe went into a convulsive mania that led to the savage ecstasy of the first Crusades. Inflamed by the Catholic Church, entire towns left their homes and began to march. The greatest example of abnormal suggestibility was seen in the Children's Crusade.[2]

No sooner had the Crusade epidemic faded than another took its place. First came the flagellants. Common men and women marched in the streets throughout Europe half naked, beating themselves in penance for the fear of God. Then came the great plagues, epidemics of physical disease that decimated whole populations, only to be followed by a wave of anti-Semitism; finally the manias known as St. Vitus' Dance and Tarantism swept the population. By the end of the fifteenth century Europe was ripe for the waves of demonophobia and witchcraft mania.[3]

During the medieval period, all aspects of life were heavily constrained, overregulated, and rigidly stratified. All the conditions were right for a mental outbreak, for when individual freedom is contained, each person to a greater or lesser degree becomes an automaton, and the suggestible, social, subwaking self comes into direct relation with molding forces in the external environment.[4]

"Applied to our time," James's notes say, "our chief lesson must be not to judge any age by the evil it contains [or] by any one of its features." Taken in its entirety, James suggests, when the "evil is ploughed under, it is the good that survives." By adopting such an attitude, we may look somewhat more dispassionately not only at our own age but also at the causes and outcome of the Inquisition.[5]

"The Inquisition, which was established in the twelfth century, helped beyond all bounds to organize belief in witchcraft," comments James. It began in the Catholic Church as a means of routing out various societies that the Church thought were propounding "heresy." Thus, James tells his audience, we saw initiated relentless persecution of "the Albigenses, the Waldenses, and the Templars." Tens of thousands of the Albigenses—a group within the Catholic Church that sought a return to the simplicity of biblical times—were massacred by Catholic priests in the twelfth century.

In his essay "Is Life Worth Living?" (1897), James referred to the persecution of the Waldenses, another sect of dissenters from the Roman Catholic Church, founded in France and Italy about 1170, and led by Peter Waldo. They too were relentlessly persecuted in the sixteenth and seventeenth centuries.[6] Similarly the Templars, a Christian society of gnostic heretics, were persecuted by the Catholic Church in the fourteenth and fifteenth centuries for their alleged ties with Manichaeanism (a religious doctrine teaching the release of the spirit from matter through asceticism), their deviation from prescribed ritual, and their worship of the Devil.

"In 1484," James goes on, "the famous Bull of Pope Innocent VIII, the *Summis Desiderantes Affectibus,* was issued which inaugurated the epidemic of witch trials that raged for a century." The bull officially appointed two Dominican monks, Heinrich Kramer and James Sprenger, to study the outbreak of witchcraft in northern Germany and, with the aid of both church and civic authorities, to effect a permanent restoration of canon law. The result of their investigation was the publication of the *Malleus Maleficarum*, or *Witches' Hammer*, in 1486. The *Malleus* went into fourteen editions between 1487 and 1520 in German, French, and Italian. Confirmed by successive popes, it became part of the body of European jurisprudence for three hundred years. It lay on the bench of every judge, the desk of every magistrate, and was accepted by both Catholic and Protestant legislators. "The Dominican inquisitors worked up the whole business," James tells his audience. "No witch was burned except in the name of the Pope—though Protestants must not throw stones [as history has shown us in] Scotland."[7]

The notes then comment: "Hold up the book" (for his audience to see). The Harvard Library Charging Records show that James frequently referred to a copy of the *Malleus* that is now in Houghton Library. This 1620 edition, in the original Latin, contains a few entries in James's characteristic penciled index on the last blank page; like most of the other copies available from that time, it is bound in thick leather covered with a thin, translucent layer of animal skin.[8]

By its appearance and its content, says James, the book "communicates a spiritual atmosphere that drips with blood," equivalent only to the "excesses of Babylonia." He then reads out to his audience a quote from Snell. Otto Snell, M.D., had published *Hexenprozesse und Geistesstörung*, his investigations comparing the alleged symptoms of the witchcraft epidemic with modern cases of hysterics, in 1891.[9] Reviewing the contents of the *Malleus*, Snell had remarked: "It is one of the most curious works which has come from the hand of man. No primeval animal, no cuneiform writing, no tool of a primitive culture will appear to us as so completely incomprehensible as this book. It is impossible to conceive that for four hundred years . . . in Germany there were people who were subject to this kind of delusion and bad judgement as well as cruelty, who stood so low as the *Malleus* proves on every page."[10]

The *Malleus*, James concurs, was an absolutely "antediluvian monster," complete with "cuneiform inscription . . . a ghostly combination of authority with feebleness of intellect." Those who wrote it combined "the powers of life and death with a mental make-up that is almost idiotic for its meanness, timorousness, and unmanliness." The authors had "a mind no bigger than a pin's head, guiding a will that stuck at nothing in the way of cruelty and conscience raised to a fever heat by the idea that the battle was directly waged with God's enemy, Satan, there in the very room. The most curious, gruesome, rathole feeling exudes from it.

"The book is a complete philosophy of witches in three parts: 1) the Devil, the witch, and the Divine permission; 2) the varieties of witches, their cures, and proofs; and 3) the procedure of extracting the confession." Though his time was short, James evidently read to his audience a selection from the table of contents of the questions he thought most pregnant:

—Whether the Belief that there are such Beings as Witches is so essential a Part of the Catholic Faith that Obstinancy [sic] to maintain the Opposite Opinion manifestly savors of Heresy.

—Why it is that there cannot be a Witch without the Devil.

—How it is that Women are Chiefly Affected.

—Of the Continuing of the Torture, and of the Devices and signs by which the judge can Recognize a Witch, and how he ought to Protect himself from their Spells. Also how they are to be shaved in those parts where they use to Conceal the Devil's Masks and Tokens; together with the due setting forth of Various means of Overcoming their Obstinancy in Keeping Silence and Refusal to Confess.

—Method of passing sentence upon one taken and Convicted, but who denies Everything.[11]

"Why were the victims mainly the poor?" James asks. "Why were they mainly women?" and "Why were the accused so much more sinful than devils, themselves?" His notes suggest that there was something lacking in the life of the "monkish" persecutors, and the fact that most of the accused were baptized suggests a Christian bias. Problems that the monks had dealing with their own vows of celibacy may have led to a hatred of the female sex and consequent persecutions.

"Whatever works" to condemn the alleged witches was used, he continues. They were accused of bringing on hail storms, ruining harvests, killing horses, and conjuring cows so that they became dry of milk. Witches, according to the *Malleus,* would "kill and eat unbaptized children" and "make their flying salve with the fat." They would also "substitute changelings," says James, alluding to an example involving three nurses. Accounts are given of children who do not cry "except when something wrong is done in the house," develop "the cough," and "die before age seven"; and finally, the witches are supposed to "aid demons to possess" others, although "this was the later subject of great debate."

The accused are further supposed to have signed a contract with the Devil and held Sabbaths, making a mock of orthodox Mass by substituting orgies and love spells. It was thought that they had the power to "change themselves into men and beasts" and to "turn other people into beasts."

They can be known, the *Malleus* continues, by certain definite signs. They "can't sweep." They "feel no pain in torture." They perform supernormal feats. They "shave their skin," and often manifest the "stigmata diaboli," or marks of the Devil, the name given to the presence of large patches of anaesthesia on different portions of the body. Here James interjects, "Our hysterics!" pointing out the obvious parallel.

The power of the witches, the book tells us, enables them to keep silent during even the most gruesome tortures. The witch supposedly effects this by certain acts, one of which James refers to in his notes with the phrase "mustn't touch the ground." The *Malleus* recounts an episode in which at the moment of a witch's capture, her would-be captors were all struck dead by lightning. For these reasons the accused was often seized and, before she could work her spell, carried out on a board or in a basket without touching the ground.[12]

The accused "mustn't see the judge first," because if she did, she might work her charms and influence the minds of her captors, who might allow her to go free.[13]

There were also definite "rules of trial," which apparently superseded those of regular criminal proceedings. The accused "may be arraigned merely by anonymous complaint," or suspicion, and without evidence. This was to be interpreted as "only a matter of custody" rather than as a form of punishment. When arraigned, the accused was allowed no advocate except one chosen by the judge. The advocate himself could be tried if he appeared to be defending heresy. "Children, wives, and husbands could testify against each other," and it was not uncommon even to torture the witness.

"The *Malleus* says that the judge may falsely promise life to get the victim's confession," James notes. " 'He won't condemn her,' the book says: 'she shall not be put to death' "; but then, of course, the judge is allowed these subterfuges. The judge also "conjures them to shed tears if innocent," since the inability to shed tears was a sure sign of the Devil. This was also a characteristic found in late nineteenth-century cases of hysteria. All of this we can plainly see, James proclaims to his audience, is "diabolically malicious!" And as a result, "the confessions rarely failed to come."

The accused was to be "interrogated and shown the instruments of torture," then confined in prison on bread and water, and visited by the hangman and others who advised her to confess. Torture was to be "continued," but "not repeated" with the same devices or in the same location twice. The book says that: "if she confesses under torture, she should then be taken to another place and questioned anew, so that she does not confess under the stress of torture. The next step of the judge should be that, if after being fittingly tortured she refuses to confess the truth, he should have other engines of torture brought before her, and tell her that she will have to endure these if she does not confess. If then she is not induced by terror to confess, the torture must be continued on the second and third day, but not repeated at that time unless there should be some indication of its probable success."[14] "The witches' Sabbath was fully described," James adds, probably giving details to his audience.

The *Malleus* was virtually a book of spiritual pornography that reflected the hysterical mania of the age. Monks who had taken a vow of celibacy depicted all the lurid details of what they were denied. Their descriptions combined reality and imagination in an officially sanctioned document, and the magistrates who used the book merely carried out what they saw as the letter of the law. A product of the sub-waking intelligence, the *Malleus* called forth the inflamed passions from the same substratum in the reader.

And what of the accused? "All were executed on sufficient evidence," James comments. He then recounts a number of specific cases from France, Germany, and Salem, Massachusetts. Among these was the case of Anna Eve.[15]

Anna Eve, while washing clothes one day in 1660 in France, reprimanded a group of unruly children playing nearby. It was later said that she had some cause to strike one of them. The child was a daughter of the local pastor. This accusation arose from the daughter herself. Sometime later, in a series of events not related to the incident, the young daughter died unexpectedly and her mother had a dream that a dragon flew into the house of the unfortunate washerwoman, Anna Eve, bewitching her. On the basis of this spectral evidence Anna Eve was arrested as a witch, accused of having caused the death of the churchman's daughter. Upon interrogation, she denied the charge, and so it was decided that torture would be applied to extract a confession.

She was asked four questions: Would she give up sorcery after having killed this child? What methods were used to kill the child? Did she have a pact with the dragon? How was this pact made with the dragon?

She answered that she would rather die than be involved in sorcery, that she was not such a woman, and that the wife of the pastor had no evidence that she was a witch. Not being a sorceress, she had no means to learn that trade. She had never seen a dragon and knew nothing about having a pact with one. Having no such pact, she had no knowledge of one. Why not ask her accusers, since they seemed to have all the details?

Torture was applied and then reapplied, while the questions were asked again in the intervals. Her reply was that she had never touched the child, that she was a good Christian, and that they were torturing her unjustly. But during the torture she continually acted as if she were crying, yet no tears came.

During the first question her hands were squeezed in a vise; during the second question her feet were pierced with spikes inserted in a pair of Spanish Boots; during the third question they used a strap on her; and during the fourth question the Boots were again applied but with more pressure.

A meeting of magistrates to discuss her case noted no tears and no complaints during torture, except for her protestations of innocence. During torture she fell asleep twice and snored loudly at one point. Her face kept good color. Concerning her imprisonment, the warden said that she had been an exceptional prisoner because she did not cry out in pain during the harshest part of the proceedings. Examining her, he was unable to find any scars. This proved her guilt beyond a doubt. His assistant added that her hunger was not diminished. Thus was her fate sealed.

More torture and questioning followed; they hung her upside down and applied the Boots, the rack, and fire to her nose and ears, whereupon she died. Just at the moment of death, a butterfly flew into the open window of the torture chamber, capturing her attention as she awakened from a swoon. Focusing on it for a long moment, she at last passed away. This last episode was duly entered into the record as evidence that she was in fact a witch, for at death she had turned herself into a butterfly and flown out the window.[16]

In this case a series of unrelated events is woven together into a causal chain by the dead girl's mother, leading to the dream and the accusation. The inability of the accuser to distinguish the dream state from waking reality plays a crucial role in the episode. Also, the types of questions put to Anna Eve suggest the predominant influence of a fixed idea in the minds of the judges. She was already guilty; she merely needed to confess. Sanctioned by social norms at the time, the accuser and the judges participated in the same delusion. As for Anna Eve, the fact that she shed no tears, remained anaesthetized to torture, maintained her hunger, and, if we are to believe the account, remained unscarred, are all characteristic hysteric symptoms, further complicated by the possibility of a dissociated state of consciousness.

The second case James cites came from evidence presented in a letter written while in prison by "John Junius."

Junius was one of five magistrates between 1627 and 1631 in Bamberg, Germany, who were accused of being warlocks and having a pact with the Devil. Curiously, the witch epidemics had subsided a number of years before these trials, but the pretext of witchcraft was revived so that the Church could confiscate the vast wealth accumulated by the accused. Junius wrote a letter to his daughter Veronica about his trial; it survived in the official records because it was never delivered. He wrote: "Innocent I have come to prison, innocent I am tortured; and innocent I will die here . . . I pray that the commissioners will interrogate my accusers under oath." But he was told, "I am afraid it will not come to pass as you like. All the judges have to do is see you." "Come now, is this evidence?" asked Junius. "You must be as little sure of me as the first honest man ever seen by you." But the judge who visited him in prison was not listening. Another judge commissioned to interrogate Junius did not come in person, but sent his son instead. Junius's chief accuser testified to seeing him dancing in the forest, but could not tell where or when. Junius's letter then described elaborate tortures—cuffs with nails, inflicting of wounds, hands crushed by pressure devices, body hung upside down and beaten with straps.

During his tortures he accused his captors of being tainted by the Devil, not himself. The devils were the torturers. This was duly entered in the record as proof of his guilt, for only the Devil himself would lay such a curse on the judges. His courage brought only more suspicion since only the Devil could effect such an attitude. Found guilty of dancing in the forest on the Sabbath, he was duly burned at the stake.[17]

Junius—himself a magistrate, the authorized voice of reason—appeared to remain in control of his faculties throughout the ordeal, while those of his tormentors appeared to be dominated by the irrational impulses of the subliminal. He maintained his innocence until the end and rightly accused his judges of being possessed. But the collective consensus of authority was against him. It was as if the collective irrational impulses of the subliminal had struck out against the puny voice of reason in one individual, claiming that right in the name of absolute truth.[18]

"Similarly," James points out to his audience, "at Salem, Massachusetts, in 1692: twenty-two were hanged; there were fifty-one confessions; and one-hundred and fifty were released. All were executed on sufficient evidence!" But "how come there was so much evidence for what *we* can't believe today?"

James's notes then refer to "Lecky"—undoubtedly the work of the Irish historian William Edward Hartpole Lecky, who wrote on the history of England and who on several occasions took up the phenomenon of the Inquisition. In his *History of the Rise and Influence of the Spirit of Rationalism in Europe* (1865), for instance, Lecky ascribed much of the witchcraft delusion not to the Devil but to lunacy.

As the waves of delusion had spread through Europe, eventually they reached the American colonies. The witchcraft superstition was brought over with the original Pilgrim Fathers. Lecky cites two in particular who were responsible for instigating the Salem epidemic: Cotton Mather and the Reverend Samuel Parris of Salem. Parris took up the persecution of his neighbors because of accusations made by his daughters, who were thought possessed; and Mather immediately wrote the history of the first year of trials and executions. It inflamed the panic already sweeping through New England, particularly because all who were skeptical of the witches' guilt were strongly denounced by public opinion and ran the risk of being persecuted themselves.[19] Lecky, an enlightened historian of his time, had called for a systematic scientific study of the Salem epidemic. In his opinion these and allied phenomena must be brought under the control of science.

James then sets forth four of the best-known theories offered at the time to account for the phenomenon of witchcraft, allegedly proven beyond a doubt by the Inquisition. First, he mentions a nineteenth-century French physician—a student of Esquirol's and author of the well-known *De la folie*—Louis Calmeil of the Montpellier Faculty of Medicine, who suggested that the signs of witches were symptomatic of a biologically based disorder. Second, he notes the theory of Jules Michelet, an eighteenth-century French historian who wrote that, "in the oppression and the dearth of every kind of ideal interest in rural populations, some safety valve had to be found." Thus Michelet believed that there really were organized secret meetings, witches' Sabbaths, and so on, to supply this need of sensation. Third, James cites Johannes Wier, a fourteenth-century writer, and Ludwig Mejer, a nineteenth-century physician, both of whom claimed that the various physical manifestations were due to the use of such potent herbs as stramonium, aconite, belladonna, herbane, and datura, commonly used as folk remedies and taken by the judges to test their alleged effects. Finally, a plausible explanation for the facts was simply the effects of torture.[20]

James then presents "Snell's refutation of the stramonium theory," based on Dr. Otto Snell's experimentation with the various drug preparations on himself, from which he reported none of the effects allegedly produced. Out of all the alleged reports of Sabbaths held, "none were actually seen," but only described hypothetically to the courts, so there were exceptions to Michelet's theory.[21] Rather, James was inexorably drawn to the conclusion that it was "not the witches, but the victim's accusers who were insane, possessed persons."

As for the victims themselves, James suggests that many were hysterics, showing that the "medical marks of witch disease" had too many parallels with recent cases to be ignored. He reminds his audience of the accusations at the beginning of his lecture that suggested hysteria, and also of more recent interpretations of the Salem epidemic. The descriptions of symptoms of possessed persons described by Constans obviously pointed to hysterics. James's notes also mention "hallucinations . . . Salem cases . . . looked at 'pinched,' " referring to frequent occasions at the Salem trials when the accused witches were asked to look at the young

girls who were their accusers. The young girls would squirm
in their seats and assert that, when the witches looked at
them, they felt as if they were being pinched by the Devil.

Such hallucinations, says James, were reported everywhere
in Europe and America. "Many of the signs assigned to
devils we now understand as hysteric symptoms, hysterical
anaesthesias particularly." So, "in the eyes of so-called enlightened criticism, we have in these accusers malicious invention. There was no *tertium quid* between possession and
fraud." The same skepticism met with in hysteria was applied
to possession: a person was perceived either as truly possessed
or as feigning the symptoms exhibited. This black and white
kind of interpretation, James says, can be seen in the "reply
of the Montpellier faculty" to questions placed before the
learned doctors by the magistrates.

Here James is referring to the fact that the magistrates of
the Inquisition in Montpellier desired confirmation of the
correctness of their condemnation and subsequent execution
of accused persons, so they presented the doctors with questions derived from their own knowledge of witches and
possession. In their reply, however, the Montpellier Faculty
members disputed every question, pointing to known medical
evidence that the same symptoms occurred in cases other than
witchcraft. Their reply was one of the major challenges to
the supremacy of the Inquisition, yet the doctors made no
attempt to explain the witches' symptoms; they only dis-
counted the questions put before them. James then read to
his audience a selection of these questions and the replies.

For instance, the Inquisitors asked if the fold produced by
curving and turning up of the body, with the head touching
the bottoms of the feet, along with other contortions and
strange postures, was a sure sign of witchcraft. The doctors
replied that mimes and acrobats do such types of strange
movements by folding and unfolding themselves in many
ways, so that medical men believed there may be no type of

posture men and women are not capable of after serious study or exercise. People are able also to execute extraordinary extensions and squaring of the limbs and other parts of the body because of the extension of nerves, muscles, and tendons; such bodily operations are only the forces of nature.

The Inquisitors asked if retarded or giddy feeling or the absence of feeling—even to the point of being pricked and pinched without complaint, without movement of the body, or change of color—were sure signs of possession. The doctors replied that there was a well-known case in which a youth let himself be eaten away by a fox, which he had hidden in his shirt, without seeming to feel; and in another case that the magistrates themselves had tried and tortured, a woman went to her death without even frowning. These cases showed that the resolute can well suffer simple pricks and pins without crying out. The doctors admitted that they were familiar with patients who showed no parts of feeling on certain areas while remaining sensitive in others. Thus, these criteria are not useful for proving possession.[22]

While the persecutions were "carried out with consummate policy and skill in acting," James points out, as far as the accused is concerned, "an honest disease was not thought of." Similarly with Upham's interpretation of the "Salem girls," says James, referring to Charles W. Upham, a Unitarian minister from Salem who attempted to investigate the witchcraft epidemic systematically. "Hysteria and all sorts of convulsions were deemed due to witchcraft and demon possession."

"The *Malleus* says that organs involved in the demon disease in question seemed healthy, the symptoms did not come from poison but became worse and not better by the doctors' remedies," James continues, prefacing that this is the opinion of the doctors themselves. He then declares, "There couldn't be a better description of functional nervous disease. It was," after all, "the doctors who [initially] invoked the devil in the Salem epidemic" by their diagnosis of a non-physical ailment. Local superstition did the rest.

"Fortunately, the doctors have got now a better understanding," adds James. "The study of hysteria, hypnotism, imitation, and all the automatisms explains in the most innocent way the phenomena, and also gives us modes of treatment more efficacious and more humane—though exorcisms also will work."

James seems to be indicating here that modern medical knowledge of the subliminal may account for much of the possession phenomena; but this does not necessarily invalidate the ability of the old-fashioned ritual of exorcism to succeed in ridding the inflicted of their malady. If anything, modern knowledge of the subconscious may even help to explain the ability of such techniques used by organized religion to undo the effect of a fixed idea.

But "this does not mean that there were no insane delusions in the witches," he concludes, citing the obvious pathology exhibited by "Tituba," the Reverend Samuel Parris's Haitian cook, who first excited the minister's daughters with the idea of possession. She openly confessed herself before the court and was hanged. The evidence also shows "occasional cases of melancholia." Nor does it exclude "Michelet's theory," that the "Black Art" and "mediumship" were not actually practiced in Paris and elsewhere. "But beyond all question," James concludes, "torture accounts for the *evidence*."

He cites a seventeenth-century work that concurred on this point, Spee's *Cautio,* which gives us a more balanced and realistic view. James's notes say only "Spee's Cautio," meaning the work of Friedrich Spee. Spee was a Jesuit and poet who was the appointed confessor of condemned witches during the persecutions at Würzburg. He heard over two hundred penitents, all of whom confided in him their innocence; yet they pleaded with him not to tell, preferring death to further torture. Spee then published an anonymous attack on the persecutions, his *Cautio Criminalis* (1631).[23] Here James's notes give the name of "Phillip von Schönborn," meaning Johann Phillip von Schönborn, patron of science, statesman, and bishop of Würzburg, who heeded Spee's call and ended the witch trials in his area.

From such works, says James, "We thus get a rational understanding of this whole nightmare episode of our race's history. In the origin a form of disease, which if rightly handled is innocent enough. But fanned and encouraged by fanatical delusion, leads to the horrors which we have seen, through medical, theological, and priestly delusion, in which whole populations shared"—all of it "made horrible beyond conception. Yet its prime agents, the friars of the Inquisition, were the most conscientious of men, the puritans of their day.

"The whole story is an example of the good intentions with which the road to hell is paved. To diminish the power of the Prince of Hell, a hell wantonly and of whole cloth was manufactured upon earth. There is no worse enemy of God and man than zeal armed with power and guided by a feeble intellect. We had it in Robespierre and the terrorists, we have it in the commune and the anarchists. The great lesson of history is to keep the power of life and death away from that kind of mind, the mind that sees things in the light of evil and dread and mistrust, rather than in that of hope.

"I have entertained you with a gloomy subject," James reflects in conclusion. "But I believe that it does one good in one's carelessness to stop now and then and realize what human life has really been, and may be again if the best of men do not keep up a constant fight, not against an imaginary Satan, but the real devil of intolerance and ignorance inflamed with the lust of power, and the conceit that they alone can save the world, by getting all the legitimate professional and legal authority into their hands.

"Strange as it may seem, there can be little doubt that a good natured skepticism and willingness to let the devil have his head a bit, is for public purposes a better state of mind than too exalted a notion of one's duty toward the world!"

: LECTURE VII :
DEGENERATION

In beginning his seventh lecture, James comments: "I now pass to degeneration. A morbid subject, but again my excuse is that looking at the facts makes the devil's sphere seem less broad and deep." By "squeezing the thistle" boldly, we rob it of its sting.[1] In other words, by bringing an unpleasant subject out into the open, we extend a more "humane view" toward the worst cases of pathology.

As for his own "enlightened age," James continues, "in law courts no *tertium quid* is recognized between insanity and sanity. If sane, a man is punished; if insane, acquitted; and it is seldom hard to find two experts who will take opposite views of his case. All the while nature is more subtle than our doctors. Just as a room is neither dark nor light absolutely, but might be dark for a watchmaker's uses and yet light enough to eat in or play in, so a man may be sane for some purposes and insane for others, sane enough to be left at large, yet not sane enough to take care of his financial affairs. The word 'crank,' which became familiar at the time of Guiteau's trial, fulfilled the need of a *tertium quid*. The foreign terms 'déséquilibré,' 'hereditary degenerate,' and 'psychopathic subject,' have arisen in response to the same need."[2]

didn't believe in intermarriage
but muth are stronger

Here James is referring first to an example still fresh in the experience of his audience, the controversy surrounding the trial, conviction, and execution of President Garfield's assassin, Charles J. Guiteau. It was probably the most celebrated insanity trial of the nineteenth century. Despite the testimony of such neurologists as George Miller Beard and William Alexander Hammond that Guiteau had a family history of insanity and that for long periods prior to the killing he had been hypermanic and had exhibited delusional ideas, dissociation, and egomania, he was judged sane and guilty of his confessed crime. Fanned by public outcry and an inflamed press, the episode demanded nothing less than the death sentence and ended with Guiteau's execution in 1882.[3]

James's point was that "human nature cannot be dealt with by these simple disjunctions." The example of Guiteau —variously labeled a "crank," with a "screw loose," "eccentric," with an "insane temperament," or "off his base," a "borderland" case whose problem was of "hereditary character"—provided a prime instance of the classification problem.

James then introduces his audience to the work of Bénédict Morel, French psychiatrist and director of the insane asylum at Saint-Yon, in southern France, who in the 1850s formulated the theory of Degeneration to explain all forms of chronic mental illness. Morel believed that mental deterioration was inherited, and that the characteristics of the degenerate were passed on from one generation to the next in a progressive pining away of the lineage until it became extinct. Thus when better stock intermarried with that which was inferior, the effect was the progressive deterioration of the race as a whole. Medical men should therefore not search for organic causes of mental illness, Morel said, but look instead into the pathological heredity of the parents.

This pessimistic theory was entirely fitted to the atmosphere of gloom and decadence that pervaded late nineteenth-century Europe.⁴ All-inclusive as it was, Morel's idea took hold and dominated French psychiatry in the 1880s. The theory then came into vogue throughout Europe, England, and to some extent in America as well.⁵ James was obviously trying to give his audience the flavor of the prevailing ideas; but he indicated that Morel's view of hereditary degeneration was simply another convenient explanation that did not cover all the facts.

So, in common parlance, there are only "two classes of mental disease, the valid and the invalid brand." A person was either normal, or if he deviated from this ideal type in any way, abnormal and therefore degenerate.

According to Morel's theory, "degeneration" applied to persons of "neurotic constitution" as well as those with "psychopathic temperament." All degenerates, Morel said, were known by definite "stigmata," in physical as well as mental characteristics. "They show fear, anger, pity, tears, and fainting," James tells his audience; they are "oversensitive" and show an "excessive response." "Unbalanced," we would call them, having "a mind discordant with itself that doesn't keep together," subject to "impulses and obsessive ideas," thus "reminding us of the conception of the integrated and non-integrated mind from which we started."

For the remainder of the lecture, James explains, we will "confine ourselves to these"—meaning the obsessions and impulsions exhibited by cases with a general nerve weakness. Such nerve weakness was then thought to be the preliminary condition out of which all the more severe disorders with their more clearly defined symptoms arose. An additional set of even more detailed lecture notes that exists for this talk labels this non-specific nervousness as "neurasthenia."⁶ James's more detailed notes begin with the "phobias of spaces, of enclosures, of crowds, of solitude, of catching a disease, of contamination," or just the generalized "fear of something dreadful, the germ of which we see in most people when they become unnerved."

"The normal germ" of pathological phobias is the momentary anxiety we experience before we seal a letter to mail it, put out the gas before leaving the house, lock a door to ward off the possibility of intruders, wind our watch to avoid missing our train, or look under the bed to make sure that the fantastic bogeyman of our childhood is not really hiding there. But "in morbid cases," he says, the idea returns insistently, again and again, despite what we do to quench the morbid feeling. He then gives some clinical examples in which the pathological idea takes the form of a "*doubt.*"

His notes allude to a patient who felt compelled to "open his mouth" repeatedly. The more detailed lecture notes attribute this example to the work of Hans Kaan, a German psychiatrist whose *Uber Beziehungen zwischen Hypnotismus und cerebraler Blutfüllung* (*The Relationship Between Hypnotism and Cerebral Blood Flow*, 1885), according to Alice Gibbens James's list, was one of the highly prized books in James's personal library.[7] But for this example, James draws from another book by Kaan, *Der neurasthenische Angstaffect* (*The Neurasthenic Affect of Anxiety*), published in 1892.[8]

The patient, who suffered from anaesthesia of the muscles around the jaws, had become fearful that he would not be able to open his mouth, and in response had developed the habit of opening and closing his mouth repeatedly whether or not he consciously wanted to do so. James says, "The act gives relief" to the patient's fear each time it is repeated, even though the effect is only temporary. "*Folie du doute,*" James called it, a nineteenth-century psychiatric classification borrowed from the French, meaning the compulsion to repeat an act that has already been successfully completed; in short, a "doubting mania."

"A good example," he goes on, "is the *recherche angoissante du mot,*" the anguish we feel in searching for a lost word. His more detailed lecture notes call for an example of "its normal germ," such as the common experience of stumbling in search of just the right word, or forgotten name, or a half-remembered fact—vague intimations of something we sense we know until we try to clarify it in the light of full consciousness.

Once he has established such a normal occurrence in the minds of his listeners, James turns to a pathological example, citing an instance from the work of Magnan. Valentin Magnan was a celebrated French medical doctor who, with Bénédict Morel, had contributed to the Degeneracy theory of mental illness.[9]

James draws his example from Magnan's *Recherche sur les centres nerveux* (1893),[10] and his lecture notes mention the case of "Georgette," a notebook, and a photograph, beginning on "page 283." On that page is described the case of a twenty-six-year-old man who developed insomnia, began to have visual and auditory hallucinations, and then became alcoholic. Within a year of the onset of these problems, he developed a need to recover lost names. During a visit to Paris, he stopped at a café, and while there read a newspaper story about a girl who had fallen into an open sewer that was being repaired. At the time he did not think much of the story. But after he returned home and retired for the night, the story came back to his mind, though he could not remember the girl's name. He could not sleep, so affected was he by his obsession to recall the girl's name. His wife, awakened by his cries of anguish, found him sitting with his head in his hands.

Suddenly he jumped out of bed sweating profusely; he said later that he had felt "squeezed," his chest had become like an oven, he could not breathe and felt as if he were suffocating. He spent the rest of the night moaning in an anxious state. When the newspaper arrived in the morning, he searched its pages until he found mention of the incident and read the girl's name, Georgette. Only then did he find relief.

The subject experienced several such occurrences. He developed the need to remember every name he heard, and so began to carry a notebook to record them. In order not to forget any, he developed an elaborate classification system for filing and cross-filing the names in his notebook. His mania also became generalized to include the forgetting of faces, so he began to collect photographs of faces in an equally morbid and compulsive manner.[11]

James's notes then mention a case of "mysophobia," or fear of contamination—a compulsion commonly observed in the form of incessant hand washing, or the wearing of gloves to protect one from touching anything related to dirt, germs, feces, and so on. Again, he draws his example from Hans Kaan's *Der neurasthenische Angstaffect.* His notes cite "page 117," a page number also written on the front cover of the book that James, in his penciled hand, described as "a classic case of washing mania."

The case was that of an eighteen-year-old girl, Fräulein V., daughter of a government official. She had inherited problems from both her mother and her father. The mother, melancholic as a girl and also affected with a washing mania, died of stomach cancer. She had inculcated in her daughter both the tendency of demanding excessive cleanliness and a special fear of dirt. At first Fräulein V. developed normally and maintained good bodily health, with the usual onset of puberty at thirteen, although, Kaan noted, she had "more goodwill than gifts."

Because of endless cleaning activities, she never got any other work done. At the beginning of puberty, she developed feelings of guilty conscience, which took the form of a fear that she did not pray and confess enough. A priest then advised her to avoid all praying. At age sixteen, she was frightened when she noticed a cancerous growth on the cheek of a woman in charge of unlocking her family's private box at the theater. After the next laundry, her handkerchief, which she had put on the railing of the theater box, came out still smelling of perfume, and the patient became convinced of infectious danger from the cancer. This led to a systematic compulsion to wash.

A gentleman she knew was bitten by a mad dog. The death that followed made in the beginning no special impression on the patient. But several years later when another friend was bitten by a healthy dog, the friend, badly mauled and bleeding, rushed into her apartment for help. The sight of him filled Fräulein V. with nameless fears. Remembering the earlier episode, she fell into another compulsive cycle and was completely given over to morbid washing. She cleaned thoroughly all the things the wounded man had come into contact with. She convinced herself that the wound was without further consequence; despite this, she retained a horror of the place where the man who had died of rabies lived, a horror that extended to the entire town and all the members of the dead man's family.

She would simulate a rabies attack whenever there was the slightest lapse in performing the cleaning compulsion. Finally, she feared even going to bed, and slept fully clothed in an easy chair. At this point, her transfer to a hospital became necessary.

The patient was completely aware that the rabies poison after many years was no longer dangerous, and further, that in her situation the danger of infection was about as likely as being hit by a meteor. Far from fearing death, she craved it as a release from her queer ideas. But in spite of all this, she was unable to overcome her fear of contracting rabies.[12]

"We see here," James's more detailed notes comment, "an obsessive idea, but no real delusion." That is to say, while the young girl appeared captivated by a fixed idea that she was contaminated, she knew intellectually that there was no basis for her fear that the cancer was infectious, or that the rabies germ could have remained viable for so many years. In other words, there was no persistent and systematic pathology of ideas, but only a single, obsessive idea. James's notes tell us that he had intended to "just mention" the case of washing mania.

James does give a detailed example of morbid desire for

counting or making calculations, called "arithmomania." First, however, his more detailed notes tell us that he gave an example of its "normal germ." How often has it happened, when we are about to get on a trolley, or make a spontaneous purchase, that we quickly count the amount of change on hand? If we are worried about the state of our finances generally, the counting may also express this more general anxiety. If we are worried that we did not bring enough cash with us, or suspect that we have been short-changed, or are worried that we may not be able to pay all our accumulated bills, we might turn over and over in our mind both the needed and the available sums.

As a pathological instance of arithmomania, James's more detailed notes refer to the counting of "spoonfuls," "mouthfuls," "appleseeds," "cherrystones," and so on, and again the notes say "Magnan on p. 281."

The case he describes concerned a young man whose malady began with an obsession for finding lost words. He, too, like the earlier subject, resorted to writing down names of people he met on the street lest he forget them. Finally he stayed isolated in his apartment, trying to avoid the problem altogether. In addition, after three months of searching for lost names, he developed an obsession for numbers. He became sad and tormented. He counted everything at the dinner table: pieces of bread, spoonfuls of water and wine, bits of meat, even the drops of milk in a spoonful and the spoons in a glassful, keeping track of it all with a blackboard he carried to the table with him.

If he ate a tomato, he had to count the seeds; the same for apples and pears. One day he was given twenty cherries but counted only nineteen pits. He kneaded feverishly through his own feces for days until he found it; only then was he able to sleep soundly. In an effort to protect himself from any unanswerable questions that might arise, he finally became a pack rat, hoarding old potato skins, bits of string, old fountain pens, and so on. Questions of infinity, Magnan wrote, particularly frightened him.[13]

The degenerate now injects a "metaphysics" into his mental operations, James tells his audience, an "infinite *Grübelsucht*" —the metaphysical tendency to brood on subtleties, which James himself at one time admitted he had suffered from in the late 1860s. Common items take on a completely different significance to the man who broods upon their nature; "oranges and apples, lemon and quince, figs and pears," and "greengage," James's notes say. He somehow used these as examples of the skepticism and unreality that too much grubbing in the abstract roots of things will breed. "Too much questioning and too little active responsibility lead, almost as often as too much sensualism does, to the edge of the slope, at the bottom of which lie pessimism and the nightmare or suicide view of life," he said in *The Will to Believe*.[14] "We have a new element here," James now points out, which produces "anxiety and dread if the idea is not obeyed." The thought, "harm will follow," is the necessary consequence of the dread feeling.

All these disorders—the *folie du doute, recherche du mot,* mysophobia, arithmomania, and the metaphysical brooding —were the classic stigmata of degeneracy, according to the "character of the scientific theory" prevailing at the time. Many authors, in taking up Morel's theory, had extended this list. It was a common trend of the times to classify nervous diseases into neat, logical categories because this rendered them somehow more scientific.

James's notes then mention "Kant's 'How is nature possible?' " Here he was referring to ideas that Immanuel Kant developed in his *Prolegomena* and *Anthropologie,* both works which James had read and commented on in 1868.[15]

To the question, "How is nature possible?", James's notes from 1868 say that Kant answers: "It is possible *materially,* through the constitution of our sense intuitions; and *for-*

mally through the constitution of our understanding, which does not draw its *a priori* from nature, but prescribes them to nature."[16] James balked at this doctrine of the supremacy of the intellect over concrete experience, and he thought a similar trend was all too plain in the field of psychopathology. Theories often counted for more than facts, and mental disorders were made to conform to categories of diagnostic classification.[17]

In a review for the *Psychological Review* (1896), James agreed with the Italian psychologist Enrico Morselli in deprecating accredited types of psychoses. "Individuals are types of themselves," James said there, "and enslavement to conventional names and their associations is only too apt to blind the student to the facts before him. The purely symptomatic forms of our classifications are based on the expressive appearances that insanity assumes according to the temper and pattern of the subject whom it affects. In short, individual subjects operate like so many lenses, each of which refracts in a different angular direction one and the same ray of light."[18]

But there can be no doubt that the drift of James's thinking here was in large part directed by his own spiritual crisis of 1870. He knew all too well that the more abstract the mental problems confronting the disturbed person, the more the feeling of existential dread intensified. Such metaphysical brooding on subtleties only intensified the feeling that "things were not right." By analogy, Kant's depressions may have resulted from a similar overintellectualized, compulsive brooding.

Although James apparently cited additional cases, the notes offer few hints. One of them, "Cowles clothing," probably refers to the work of Edward Cowles, who in 1896 was superintendent of the McLean Asylum at Waverly, the mental hospital associated with the Massachusetts General Hospital and Harvard Medical School.[19] It is reasonable to assume that James described a patient whom Cowles had presented to the Boston Medico-Psychological Society in 1885 as a classic case of doubting mania. Cowles's paper was on *folie du doute,* which he described as a form of hypochondria characterized by fixed ideas and "constrained impulsive affections," in which the patient was fully conscious of his or her morbid condition.

Cowles's case concerned M.F., a single woman, age twenty-nine, who as a child had often feared harm might come to her in consequence of doing some simple act, an idea that may have resulted from severe typhoid fever followed by a tedious and complicated recovery. M.F. became jealous of one of her schoolmates and intimate friends, C.D., because of her beauty. The jealousy soon developed into a feeling of hatred, and M.F. entertained thoughts of harmful events that might happen to C.D. She became doubly tormented as she thought of her own possible suffering from the blame that would come if the event happened.

M.F. found a way to allay these painful feelings by substituting some other person as the victim of the imagined events. It soon became necessary to substitute a person completely opposite to C.D., then to have a number of such persons, to be thought of in a certain order. After a while this set failed to give relief, and a new set of persons had to be chosen, to wear out in their turn. It was during this period that she developed troubled feelings of hesitation in performing even the simplest of acts, such as dressing, when she would put on and take off each garment many times before she could let it stay on. Other acts had to be repeated in the same way. She associated them with fear of harm to C.D. if she did not obey the morbid impulse.[20]

At this point, James's more detailed set of lecture notes also gives a somewhat ambiguous reference to an article in the *American Journal of Insanity,* cited only by page number. On that page for 1896, G. Stanley Hall was reviewing courses taught at Clark University that defined psychology as a science, and mentioned Cowles's work on cases of phobia and the compulsions, but he gave no further details.[21]

In a much earlier issue of the same *Journal,* however, a case of mania accompanied by a well-developed delusional system is presented on the cited page, an instance that agrees quite well with the flow of James's ideas in the present lecture. It was an account of testimony given at the trial of Captain John Windsor for the murder of his wife—whom he thought had plotted against him—in 1850.

Windsor, a merchant, had married his second wife when he was seventy years old and she was twenty-four. Within a few months she became pregnant. Already old and decrepit, and prone to superstitions and delusions of the senses, Windsor soon developed severe delusions. He believed that his wife had been unfaithful, that the child she was carrying was not his but that of a neighbor; that the wife saw the neighbor frequently in secret meetings, giving him money she had pilfered from her husband's cash register; and that she was responsible for drawing other unnamed persons into a plot to poison him.

The idea of attempted poison developed when he began reporting burning sensations on his arms, head, and nose. He soon came to believe that his wife had filled his bed and clothes with the poison, and so was found one day "whipping the poison out of his clothes" with a cow-skin (piece of leather). An employee had also witnessed him performing an elaborate ritual in the stables, where he drew some pictures and shot at them with a gun in one hand while holding a Bible in the other. Windsor then took the pictures to his smokehouse, burned them, carefully wrapped up the ashes, and commanded the employee to throw the parcel into a running brook. He had extracted the procedure, he explained, from the Bible, and his purpose in going through the ritual was to "stop the conjuration and witchcraft."

Two weeks later, after mistaking his own and his son's

footprints for those of his wife and neighbor, and believing them to have made another secret rendezvous. Windsor approached his wife with a pistol while she was weaving, shot her, and then tried to commit suicide with laudanum.[22]

"Page 240" of the text refers to the conclusion that Windsor was obviously under the influence of a diseased imagination, arising out of delusions that had immediate effect on the act he committed. These delusions completely subjugated the power of his will, assuming an influence over his mind that was much greater than the weight of normal ideas. Such systematized delusions, revolving as they do around a central idea, define the medical condition known as monomania.

"Observe," James tells his audience, how "harm [can come] to a person by thought conjured by other thoughts, or other persons," all woven into a complicated system. Note also, he points out, the "exorcism" and the effect of the ritual on a temporary "cancelling" of the impulsive dread. "All sorts of devices" are resorted to, he says. Here he mentions two additional cases, published by a French doctor, Henri Legrand du Saulle, and a Dutch doctor, Frederick Van Eeden, respectively.

James's notes cite the case of "pretty women" given in Legrand du Saulle's *La Folie du doute, avec délire du toucher*.[23] This was the case of a sixty-year-old man who commenced to feel, when sixteen years old, an aberration of mind that never ceased over a forty-four-year period. When he went to the theater, he returned tormented by the desire to know all about the actresses he had seen. He wanted to know their birthplace, family, age, their habits, and the manner of their life. This desire was so lively and persistent that it constituted a fixed idea. It distressed him so much that he gave up going to the theater; but soon his curiosity, in place of relating only to actresses, was aroused in meeting any woman whom he thought pretty.

The man concealed his fixed idea, followed the profession

he had taken, and married; but the fixed idea remained. Whenever he saw a woman whom he thought good-looking, he was in an anxious condition for hours. Finally he retired from business and his condition gradually began to improve of itself. But whenever he went out, he had to be accompanied by a person who was able to reassure him about all the women he met. He always put the same question: "Is she pretty or not?" His companion would answer that she was plain, and the compulsion would immediately leave him.

Such ordinary precautions were not always able to avert unexpected crises, which would then have their effect for several hours. At last the man ventured out only at night. On one occasion he went on a night train. After traveling thirty-five miles, he asked if the woman who gave him his ticket was pretty or not. His companion, being fatigued, uncautiously said that she had not noticed and could not really say. He fell into a great fit of distress. Someone was immediately dispatched to go and look at the ticket woman. The messenger returned shortly, presumably without ever seeing her, and reported that she was very ugly.[24]

The example James cites from Van Eeden, the Dutch physician and psychotherapist,[25] concerned a young man who feared that if he did not touch once more a certain stone, see once again a certain person, or revisit a certain house, something dreadful would happen to him.[26] Over a twenty-year period, for instance, he made a pilgrimage every Sunday afternoon to a certain railroad station to hit a certain light pole three times with his right foot, then three times with his left foot. If he did not do this, he feared his father would die. When his father finally died of old age, the man quit the behavior.

Still he would travel thirty kilometers just to touch a pebble he had seen before. He permitted himself to eat only an odd but not an even number of potatoes. Friday and Saturday he wore only a certain colored tie. He avoided certain streets. Each day he read a certain number of newspapers completely through from first word to last for fear that, if he did not, something would happen.[27]

Such a case, James's detailed notes say, "shades into general anxious melancholy" and involves disturbances of the rational functions. "Different are the pure motor impulses where the act is primarily the thing suggested." Morbid thoughts are not involved. Surprisingly, in these cases the intellectual functions, to whatever level they are developed, appear to remain intact. "We have the so-called manias" as examples of this purely motor impulse: "dypsomania," the irresistible obsession to drink; "kleptomania," the impulse to steal; "pyromania," the uncontrollable urge to set fires, found "mostly in imbeciles"; "suicidal and homicidal manias," in other words the impulse to kill oneself or others. "All of them show great trouble, though they exist in germinal form in the healthy personality."

James then points out the streak of kleptomania in all of us: "We pay for the goods at the desk, but our will is overpowered with the momentary thought to steal all the same." The only difference between the normal person and the kleptomaniac is that the normal person recovers control almost immediately before the act is done, whereas the kleptomaniac irresistibly performs the act once it has been suggested.

He follows this with an example of "oniomania," or the pathological condition of money-spending, pointing out that any of us may at some time have engaged in a money-spending spree or at least cultivated the fantasy of doing so. This was the normal germ of the more aggravated disturbance.

Suicide, a dreadful thought for most of us, except when it may have suggested itself in a particularly low and painful moment, is of two kinds, James's notes say: "the sudden impulse," as in the case of "the musician the other day" (referring to a local case in his experience); or the long, slow, and deliberate act that the person has brooded on incessantly until there is no other choice but to go ahead. This second form is often accompanied by long depression, and more than one attempt may have been made.[28]

Next, James goes on to consider an instance of homicide. His more detailed notes show that he drew this example from a doctoral thesis presented to the Faculty of Medicine of Paris in 1882 by Gabriel Descourtis.[29] James's notes refer to "page 23," and signaled by his characteristic marginal marks is the example of homicidal mania—the case of a husband who killed his children in despair over the earlier death of his wife.

"I will say nothing of those blood-thirsty types, safe to say," James tells his audience, cases such as "Jack the Ripper," who suffer from morbid impulses compounded by "cruelty in general, moral insanity, and anti-social impulses." Usually, but not always, they suffer from "weakness of intellect," which they make up for with brute cunning. "But weakness of intellect [may be] still greater in pure motor impulses." He then gives an example of simple tics, where no amount of will exerted can control the behavior. At this point his more detailed notes introduce the complex case of impulse mania drawn from Prichard.

James Cowles Prichard, a Scottish medical doctor and ethnologist, was best known for identifying the class of mental disorders that he called moral insanity. Prichard essentially challenged the prevailing psychiatric notion of his time, which stated that insanity always affected the faculty of reason. He showed the prevalence of insanity that involved only the emotions and behavior, while the intellect of the patient remained quite intact. Many of these cases involved no delusions or hallucinations, formerly the main legal criteria for judging a person insane.[30]

James's detailed notes refer to a case on "page 42–3," where there is a light pencil mark next to a case of impulsive behavior in an insane man. This man, free on his own recognizance from the asylum, had the singular habit of opening his window at a certain hour every night and crying out *"murder"* exactly twelve times. He would also go every day after dinner into the middle of the quadrangle near his bedroom and throw his hat into the air a precise number of times, shouting at each throw. It was discovered that his motive for acting thus was a notion that by consistency and uniformity of conduct, he afforded proof of his sanity. He lived for many years on his estate, where his conduct, though eccentric and not that of a sane man, was without injury to himself or others.[31]

"There is no end to the possible kinds of obsession," James tells his audience; "the anti-vivisectionist mania, the anti-slavery mania, the unity of Italy mania. . . ." And he cites a case of bathing mania reported by Hugo Münsterberg, James's colleague in experimental psychopathology at Harvard.[32]

There are even "cases of love-mania" reported by Danville. Gaston Danville, a French author, had written *La Psychologie de l'amour* in 1894, which James had checked out of the Harvard College Library in the fall of that same year. The only copy of the work now available at Harvard, at the Medical School, contains marginal marks in it. Although there is no corroborating evidence that the marks belong to James, their style suggests that they may be his.[33]

Often, says James, life is seen as evoking a challenge from certain individuals, who feel themselves to be fittest to answer in a "superior" way. We all know of such "one idea-d" persons, he goes on, naming more than a half dozen then currently in the minds of his audience—Henry Berg, founder in 1866 of the American Society for the Prevention of Cruelty to Animals; Charles Henry Parkhurst, Presbyterian clergyman and reformer, who held a New York City pastorate from 1880 to 1918, and who launched a furious attack on organized crime in state government, which led to an official investigation; Dorothy Dix, mid-nineteenth-century humanitarian who visited the insane asylums and forced legislation for improvement of the care for the mentally ill; John Brown, famous abolitionist before the Civil War, who led the raid on Harper's Ferry; General Booth, founder of the Salvation Army; Frances Willard, president of the World Woman's Christian Temperance Union, suffragette, and founder of the Prohibition Party in 1883; and others.

Here is "our transition to genius," James notes. "These persons are not *insane,* not maniacs, not melancholics, not deluded; yet they are not sane." They are "monomaniacs," free in the world because they can still function. But they are "mattoids"—Lombroso's term for those pseudo-geniuses who are deformed slightly from the normal because "they have divided selves." They can't control their one reigning and glorious impulse. Yet when we examine them in detail, James says, "they show under a microscope the play of human nature." They teach us about "ideas and their associations, all such ideas being impulsive or inhibitive." We call them geniuses but they are not; they are "déséquilibrés"— out of balance. Their "horses" have gone out of control of the "driver."

"All such people who feel challenged may tend to genius. The question is why certain ideas are so strong as to coerce their attention; why such associations are formed—such emotions as doubt, wonder, or fear. When their actions are *bad* enough, we pity them; elsewhere we blame them," especially the "irresolute types suffering from delirium and negation.

"In some cases," James concludes, "we begin to know where the ideas come from." We see the non-specific anxiety, and the attempt at relief. It appears that "a certain process vibrates independently"; but "whence its source?" The success of "post-hypnotic suggestion" in many instances "reminds one of the fixed ideas we saw in hysteria and demon possession." But as yet, these ideas from the new experimental psychology of the subconscious have not been applied to the most severe cases of insanity; by so doing there may be renewed hope for those now looked upon as incurable.

: LECTURE VIII :

GENIUS

"The prevailing opinion of our time," declares James in opening his final lecture, "supposes that a psychopathic constitution is the foundation for genius." Such was the temperament of persons controlled by one idea, as with "Dr. Parkhurst, Frances Willard, and Lady Somerset."[1] His point is that while such individuals may appear before the public eye as geniuses, in reality they are "mattoids," pseudo-geniuses, because they are controlled by a single unconscious impulse and no other element in their make-up contributes to their acclaim. In fact, there could be as many of these pseudo-geniuses as there are single ideas to latch onto. "There is no end to *these* kinds of people,"[2] he says, "which leads us to the question of [just what then really constitutes] genius."

"Myers explains it," James's notes say, "by an 'uprush' of contents from the subliminal." Genius, F. W. H. Myers had claimed, should be regarded as the power of utilizing a wider range than other men can utilize of faculties in some degree innate in all; a power of appropriating the results of subliminal mentation to subserve the supraliminal stream of thought. Thus an inspiration of genius will be in truth a *subliminal uprush*, an emergence into the current ideas which a man is consciously manipulating of other ideas he has not consciously originated, but which have shaped themselves beyond his will, in the profounder region of his being. Myers stressed that there is no real departure from normality; that is to say, no abnormality at least in the sense of degeneration, but rather a fulfillment of the true norm of man, with the suggestion of something *supernormal,* of something that transcends existing normality, as an advanced stage of evolutionary progress transcends an earlier stage.[3]

"But turn now to another view of genius," remarks James, the classical, academic perspective, where genius is thought to be "divine, miraculous, and God-given." Such a person would have "no meanness, and no selfishness." He would be the perfect "effulgence of light." We should "adore" him; meanwhile, it would be utter "blasphemy to critically analyze such a view.

"Contrast this with the more realistic tendency," the notes go on, where science has shown genius to be historically allied with morbidity. "Not only are we blots against the sun, but the sun also is itself a blot" against the larger universe. The view is relative, in other words. Modern medical science has put the classical, idealized, and uncritical view of genius in better perspective. Yet the scientific view itself errs by making the same kind of absolute assertion, based as it was on an incomplete consideration of the facts.

James then cites L. F. Lelut, Jacques-Joseph Moreau, Cesare Lombroso, and John F. Nisbet as proponents of the prevailing medical view that genius was allied with degenerative insanity.[4] He had studied the work of these authors intensively in the early 1890s in preparation for his graduate lectures in mental pathology at Harvard. His conclusions on their theories of Degeneracy and Genius were published in the *Psychological Review* for 1895, and major portions of that article found their way into this lecture on "Genius" a year later. These conclusions were to be set forth once again in the *Varieties* in 1902.[5]

James begins with a critique of Lelut's book, *Du Démon de Socrate* (1836).[6] The formula was quite straightforward, says James ironically. Someone who is "visionary" is called a "halluciné," and the presence of hallucinations means madness. "Forgetting that it is Socrates who is in question," he tells his audience, "turning from the greatness of the name and seeing only the reality of the fact, following imperturbably the chain of my deductions, passing from one term in the formula to another by a purely algebraic process: $a = b$, $b = c$, $c = d$, therefore $a = d$, I arrive at the definitive equation 'Socrates = madman.' All because he once stood motionless for many hours in the cold and spoke of having a guiding demon.

"Even if by this demon were really meant hallucinations of hearing, we know now that one in eight or ten of the population has had such an experience and that for insanity we must resort to other tests than these." James's meaning here is clear: that inner events in any form are denigrated to the level of pathology by the normal, externally oriented, predominantly verbal attitude of medical science. Medicine should have adopted a more enlightened attitude toward such events.[7]

"But the ball was set rolling in 1859 by Moreau, who showed psychopathic heredity in genius with many cases." Moreau's point, according to one of his followers, emphasized that genius was essentially a nerve affection, his contention being that originality of thought and quickness of intellectual faculties were originally similar to madness and idiocy. All of which goes to show, James points out to his audience, that "madness ferments in the dough of which great men are made." But "madness and genius are congeries," a heap or a aggation of mental qualities that may or may not have a direct relation. Here James suggests again what he refers to as Myers's Problem—the fact that the best that is within us seems to express itself to consciousness through the same channels as the worst, thereby causing us to confuse the two. *"In radice convenient,"* says James; they appear to come together at their root.

James's notes then cite an illustration from Moreau's *La Psychologie morbide*, in which the correlations of cranial measurements of geniuses were compared with those of idiots and imbeciles, showing a similarity. James's copy of this work is autographed, and contains both marginal marks and the characteristic penciled index at the end.[8] The index refers to several cases, but there is no corroboration from the lecture notes as to which ones he gave to his audience. His notes do show a reproduction of Moreau's schematic diagram (opposite), which allegedly demonstrates the graphic relation between geniuses and other degenerative types.

James then proceeeds to give an explanation of Moreau's chart: "There are six branches to the tree. Insanity proper, paralysis, spasmodic and neuralgic affections, psychopathy, and genius. On the left we see bodily diseases, anaesthesias, neuralgias, epilepsy, spasmodic disorders, hysteria, paralysis, tumors of the brain, and so on. On the right mental branches we see idiocy at the bottom, then insanity proper, then eccentrics and impulsives, utopists, criminals, cranks, and finally geniuses at the top."

Such was the type of classification of mental disease prevalent in James's time, usually idiosyncratic to the particular cases observed by the promulgator of the system, based on subjective impressions, and guided by the particular models dominating the science of the period.

Next, James refers to Lombroso, "who squarely calls geniuses degenerate," and places genius "near the epileptic variety."[10] The creative power of genius, Lombroso said, may be a form of degenerative psychosis and belong to the family of epileptic affections.

Then James quotes Nisbet's *The Insanity of Genius* (1891): "Within the past few years science has opened up new methods of inquiry, thrown new light upon many cognate

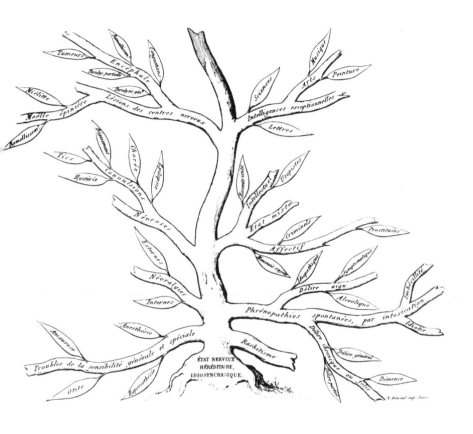

J.-J. Moreau's Classification of Mental Disorders

subjects, and placed new instruments in the hands of the investigator for getting at the truth. The results of modern research affecting most intimately the question of genius are, first, the localization of the functions of the brain, and secondly, the established kinship of an extensive group of brain and nervous disorders, of which insanity or paralysis is the more obvious expression, and gout, consumption, malformation, etc., the more obscure. Both these branches of knowledge are of greatest utility in solving the problem before us, and their dire application to the facts of biography will be found to rob genius of some, if not all, of the mystery which has hitherto enshrouded it.

"The result is to place upon a solid basis of fact the long suspected relationship of genius to insanity. Apparently at opposite poles of the human intellect, genius and insanity are, in reality, but different phases of a morbid susceptibility of, or want of balance in, the cerebrospinal system."[11]

Nisbet went on to say that this conclusion was arrived at from a close examination of the lines of the greatest men whose personal family history was authentically known. He even asserted that he, indeed, had been under no temptation to trim or square the facts, for whenever a man's life was at once sufficiently illustrious and recorded with sufficient fullness to be a subject of profitable study, that person inevitably fell into the morbid category—"a remarkable proof," said Nisbet, "of the soundness of the theory which after all need not, like a chain, be tested by its weakest link."[12] So geniuses, "without exception," Nisbet concluded, are insane.

James also cites another author, Max Nordau, who likewise asserted that genius is allied with "hysteria," as shown by the characteristic "invasion" of psychic contents, as well as such other symptoms as insomnia.[13]

"The methods of proof" used by these experts are "very simple," says James. "There is first the history of morbidity in the family to consider; second, the history of the genius himself; and third, the mortality" among geniuses stemming from neuropathic diseases. Using these criteria, "it is astonishing how many persons you can show to have had some nervous trouble," he tells his audience.

James's notes enumerate "Lombroso's list of eccentricities that accompany both genius and degeneration." James apparently began by describing Lombroso to his audience, with the implication that Lombroso himself justly fitted his own description. Lombroso's book mentions "short stature, rickets, leanness, odd physiognomy—unlike their parents or the normal types of their nationality, anomalies of the skull and brain, stammering, left-handedness, impulsiveness, somnambulism, flights of inspiration, double personality, stupidity in other matters, over-sensibility, forgetfulness, originality, word-coining, epilepsy, melancholia, delusions of conceit and greatness, doubting mania, drunkenness, hallucinations, no moral sense, and longevity"—this last meaning that their length of life was usually short.

Lombroso's theory was that "genius is a degenerative neurosis allied with epilepsy and moral insanity. Dante, Michelangelo, and Guido had been thrown at him as examples who were normal," James had said of those authors in his 1895 review. "But Lombroso proves minutely their strongly eccentric and neurotic constitution. Dante, in particular, must have been frankly epileptic, for no less than eleven times in the Divine Comedy, he speaks of himself as swooning or falling unconscious. Lombroso goes on to say that the weakness of genius cannot be due to secondary strains and fatigues incidental to the ardent sort of life which the possession of greatness imposes; [such] is proved by the fact that out of three-hundred and thirteen symptoms of fatigue which Lombroso has counted, only six are commonly found among geniuses." James then names these symptoms: "somnambulism, pallor, impracticality, helplessness, irritability, and depressed spirits."

Lombroso also showed "the frequency of degenerative anomalies in geniuses. For example, they vary from their national type as proved by portraits. Longfellow, Bellamy, Tennyson, Coleridge look like men of Latin race. Darwin and Bryant, Coleridge and Burns, George Eliot and Bulwer form mutually resembling pairs. 'The cause of these resemblances,' Lombroso says, 'is to be sought in the degeneration common to them all.'

"Professor Lombroso," James continued his review, "has compared the field of view of twelve geniuses of his acquaintance with that of eight unusually gifted men who were not geniuses, and found a shrinkage of the inner upper quadrant in nine of the geniuses—in none of them was the field symmetrical. The non-geniuses were much more normal; so that an abnormal field of view seems to characterize geniuses, he concludes. Among the other *bizarreries* of genius, playing with orthography is also mentioned, and a dog-Latin letter of Swift's to Stella is quoted. One is tempted to find in this a tendency to fabricate a jargon, a trait connecting geniuses with criminality." Indeed, in his dealings with genius, Lombroso appears to have had "more fun than a goat."[14]

Another author, John F. Nisbet, "has dealt with some two-hundred and fifty cases of genius." James quotes him as saying: "Selected upon no other ground than their eminence in the first instance, the total number of these are found to be neuropathic, suffering from, or dying of, some description of nerve disorder." Nisbet had compared these geniuses to the Registrar-General's census in England for 1888, a document that reported the proportion of deaths from the chief constitutional or nerve diseases per million population of deaths.[15] "[Max] Nordau, in his study, *Degeneration and Genius* (1890), likewise cites numerous symptoms of morbidity in Wagner, Ruskin, Ibsen, Tolstoi, Zola, Morris, and the pre-Rafaelites."[16]

"Thus when all is stated," James goes on, "we have a formidable indictment of the classic, flawless, superhuman

view. By ferreting, prying, by playing the part of the devil's
advocate," we arrive at the conclusion that "a concrete view of
human nature is superior." Yet, he suggests, the scientists
themselves have gone to the often misleading extreme.[17]

"To begin with, no essential connection between geniuses
and morbidity is proved by the methods of these authors. The
simple enumeration of geniuses with psychopathic traits, to
prove the essential pathology of all geniuses (apart from the
fact that by the same logic one could prove that being born
on a Sunday, or having brown eyes, or living in odd numbers,
was genius' essential condition), is carried out with no pre-
tense of exactitude. Rightly used, the statistical argument
ought to ascertain, first, the percentage of the mentally unsound in a given population at a given moment; then the total
number of geniuses, and finally the number of mentally
diseased geniuses, in the same population at the same
moment. If the percentage of disease were higher in the
geniuses than in the population, the neurosis theory of genius
would receive presumptive support. It is needless to say that
such statistics are unattainable, nor are they attempted by
any of the advocates of the neurosis theory.[18]

"The only attempt to use statistics methodically by advocates of the theory is in Nisbet's comparison of the causes of
death in genius and the population at large. . . .[19] He
enumerates amongst the chief constitutional or nerve diseases: phthisis, pneumonia, apoplexy, heart disease, scrofula,
rheumatism, syncope, diabetes, gout, and stone, and then tells
us that the death rate of the nerve diseases, thus Pickwickianly
understood, to the entire death rate of Great Britain in 1888,
was at 1 to 3½, whilst among the men of genius enumerated
it is at least three times greater.[20]

"Ignoring the ridiculousness of Mr. Nisbet's classification
of nerve diseases, and assuming that all of the two-hundred
and fifty geniuses really did die of them, not the total population, but some part of the population whose pursuits are
intellectual was the proper term of comparison. If Mr.

Nisbet had looked up the percentage and family history of two-hundred and fifty occupants of offices in the city, or of the two-hundred and fifty active businessmen, and found less gout and apoplexy than in his geniuses, it would have been a really interesting fact, for these are diseases of sedentary life as such and geniuses are on the whole of the sedentary class."[21]

So sedentary men provided the right terms of comparison. "The names of Emerson, Longfellow, Lowell, Whittier, and Oliver Wendell Holmes would probably be those first written by anyone who should be asked for a list of geniuses of the community of which I write,"[22] James tells his audience. He had referred to this same community in his 1880 address at Harvard on "Great Men, Great Thoughts, and the Environment": "I may be pardoned for taking so present and personal an example. I should like to use our own community as a means of illustrating my point. It seems to me that nothing proves so clearly the fact that no social community *need*, by virtue of its social forces, evolve fatally in the direction of its own most characteristic aptitudes. It is a commonplace remark that the intellectual preeminence which Boston so long held over other American cities is slowly passing away. Webster and Choate, Channing and Parker, Howe and Garrison, Prescott and Motley, Thoreau, Hawthorne, and Margaret Fuller, Jackson and Warren, Mann and Agassiz, are gathered to their fathers. Emerson and Holmes, Longfellow and Whittier, have passed their seventieth birthdays, and the new stars which are rising above the horizon are few in number, and hardly of the same order of magnitude with those that have sunk or are sinking to its verge. . . . [But] no positive condition is present which could prevent Boston from [again] becoming, if the means were given, as radiant a focus of human energy as any place of its size in the world."[23]

James was, of course, referring both to members of his father's literary circle and to other Boston personalities whom he knew personally. Emerson was a godfather and close family friend who had helped to launch William James on his literary career; Longfellow and Lowell were Harvard poets; and Oliver Wendell Holmes, the famous poet-physician, had been James's mentor at Harvard Medical School.

"Although belonging to the class of poets (the species of genius most akin to psychopathy by the sensibility it demands)," James comments, "these men were all distinguished for balance of character and common sense. So Schiller, so Browning, so George Sand. In poets like Shelley, Poe, de Musset, on the other hand, we have all the intellectual and passionate gifts without powers of inhibition. In the sphere of action we have a similar diversity of mixture; we find the all-around men like Washington, Cavour, and Gladstone; the great intellects and wills with no hearts, like Frederick the Great; the intense hearts and wills with narrow intellects, like Garibaldi and John Brown; the stubborn wills with mediocre hearts and intellects, like George III or Phillip II; and finally, the real cranks and half-insane fanatics, often with much of the equipment of effective genius except a normal set of ideas! It all depends on the mixture; only as the elements vary independently, the chances that a freak of nature in the line of human greatness will be as exceptionally strong in all three elements of character as he is in any one of them, is small. Hence some lop-sidedness in almost all distinguished personages, hence the rarity of Dantes, Saint Bernards, and Goethes among the children of men."[24]

"But if there is no necessary connection with morbidness, then why is there so frequent a connection?" James asks. "To answer that, look at ourselves! Genius is not a homogeneous conception. The only conclusion [is] that there are no incompatibles in human nature, and that any random combination of mental elements that can be conceived may also be realized in some individual."[25]

"For the purposes of Lombroso genius means any such eminence as will get a person's name into a biographical dictionary. But what is the affinity between Bonaparte and Paganini; Jay Gould and Shelley; Rockefeller and Mark

Twain; Sarah Bernhardt and Washington; Saint Paul and Rudyard Kipling? [Genius] is a social conception. To make it psychological we have to bring it down to the intellect—first class originality of intellect! Narrowed in this way, Professor [Alexander] Bain's description of it, as an unusual tendency to associate by similarity, will stand firm.[26]

"Some people are far more sensitive to resemblances, and far more ready to point out wherein they consist, than others are. They are the wits, the poets, the inventors, the scientific men, and the practical geniuses. *A native talent for perceiving analogies* is reckoned by Professor Bain, and by others before and after him, as *the leading fact in genius of every order*."[27]

Of this consciousness on the part of the genius, James had said in 1880: "But turn to the highest order of minds, and what a change! Instead of thoughts of concrete things patiently following one another in a beaten track of habitual suggestion, we have the most abrupt cross cuts and transitions from one idea to another, the most rarefied abstractions and discriminations, the most unheard of combinations of elements, the subtlest associations of analogy; in a word we seem suddenly introduced into a seething cauldron of ideas, where everything is fizzling and bobbing about in a state of bewildering activity, where partnerships can be loosened or joined in an instant, treadmill routine is unknown, and the unexpected seems the only law. According to the idiosyncrasy of the individual, the scintillations will have one character or another. They will be sallies of wit and humor; they will be flashes of poetry and eloquence; they will be constructions of dramatic fiction or of mechanical device, logical or philosophical abstractions, business projects, or scientific hypothesis, with trains of experimental consequences based thereon; they will be musical sounds, or images of plastic beauty or picturesqueness, or visions of moral harmony. But whatever their differences, they will all agree in this, that their genesis is sudden and, as it were, spontaneous. That is to say, the same premises would not, in the mind of another individual, have engendered just that conclusion; although, when the conclusion is offered to the other individual, he may thoroughly accept and enjoy it, and envy the brilliancy of him to whom it first occurred."[28]

"But," James's 1896 lecture notes say, "in the permutations of human nature this [intellect] may combine with any state of health or nerve, or temperament. Steady men or men of moods. Eager, ambitious men or lazy men. Ones with feeling; conscience or none, pertinacity or fickleness, love of self or humility. This being the case, which man is likely to get into the biographical dictionary? Those who in addition to intellect, have zeal, ambition, and doggedness. *These alone* with good enough intellect will get a man in. We all know mediocre intellects who impress their time on public affairs; such persons as Bismarck and Cleveland are notorious. One idea'd men, by that fact alone get in. Like Garibaldi or John Brown."

In other words, ideas by themselves are not enough. A psychological definition is good only insofar as it defines genius descriptively through the intellect alone. "Bain's definition," James affirms, "is truly psychological; *but it carries no consequences.*"[29] Here James was expressing the full force of his soon to be unveiled doctrine of pragmatism. A genius may have many creative ideas, a pseudo-genius only one; the common fact between them, however, is that ideas lead to concrete effects, and it is for those effects that a person is ultimately remembered.

"Maniacs are due to lack of inhibition; degenerates' obsessions are not original in this sense. Liability to obsessions, excessive sensibility, and impulsivity are, however, conditions of *effective* genius" when combined with superior reason, powerful imagination, and a strong will.[30] "Even though geniuses are liable to obsession, they work it off through their socially constructive efforts. Psychopathic temperament then does not *constitute*" genius, for "most psychopaths have weak intellects. But when a powerful intellect is psychopathic *as well* . . . it [becomes] more probable that he will make his mark and affect his age, than if his temperament were less neurotic.[31]

"In the artistic life we also see the excessive sensibility of the psychopath," James says. "Everywhere the haunting doubts, arrangements . . . number combinations; the search for what is lost; the metaphysics; the moral intensity; the belief in a mission." Here James refers to some example in his own experience involving "hymn books." "Public opinion restricts [its definition] of genius to *artistic* genius, and even there to capriciousness," which we see as "romantic rather than classical." But "even within the artistic temperament there are immense differences of type. So the neurosis theory of genius is in one sense true, but not in that way in which the contemporary authors mean it,"[32] meaning that geniuses may have nervous instability, but it may be adaptive, rather than pathological as most authors claim.

James points out one very distinguished exception to the genius authors in "Hirsch's book." William Hirsch's *Genie und Entartung (Genius and Degeneration)* was first published in German in 1894, and was translated into English anonymously by Charles Sanders Peirce in 1896.[33] Peirce praised Hirsch for his broader scientific approach, though he also noted that Hirsch, who was a clinician, even an alienist, wrote in "tiresome, repetitious, and gelatinous sentences."[34]

James's copy of Hirsch's *Genie und Entartung* is extensively marked, especially the chapters on the psychology of genius and genius and insanity. James considered Hirsch to be the most eminently readable of all the genius and degeneration authors, and the one who presented the most balanced view. James and Hirsch agreed that there was no single acceptable standard among philosophers, scientists, or literary men that accurately defined genius. For if genius is to be defined by any character of the mind, they both said, its conception must be constructed and defined from within, and cannot be dependent on outward circumstances. In other words, the determinants of genius rest solely within the individual, though the criteria for effective genius are in terms of outward results.[35] "So one more lurid, picturesque and smoky idea [is now] gone!" remarks James.

"But let us look back now. We have taken many lurid things and made them tamer. Hypnotism equals sleep. Hysteria with all its symptoms equals hypnotism. Double personality simply concerns the buried idea that collects experiences until it assumes an apparently independent form. Demon possession equals an optimistic mediumship. Witchcraft is explained simply as mass hysteria over neurotic symptoms. And finally, we know that insane genius, while perhaps more romantic, now flattens out.

"The result is to make disease less remote from health. And health is basically an affair of balance. Even if one leg is shorter than the other, yet in all respects both continue to grow naturally, then we still class it as a diseased member. No *one* thing can make a man sound or unsound. Susceptibilities and obsessions, on the contrary, when found in creative geniuses such as Goethe or Gladstone, only prove the universality of the rule. The line of health is not narrow! A peculiarity then, when it is recognized, should be welcome if it can be made useful."[36]

"There is a strong tendency among these pathological writers I have cited," James had said in 1895, "to represent the line of mental health as a very narrow crack, which one must tread with bated breath, between foul fiends on the one side and gulfs of despair on the other. Now health is a term of subjective appreciation, not of objective description, to borrow a nomenclature from Professor [Josiah] Royce; it is a teleological term. There is no purely objective standard of sound health. Any peculiarity that is of use to a man is a point of soundness in him, and what makes a man sound for one function may make him unsound for another. Moreover we are all instruments for social use, and if sensibilities, obsessions and other psychopathic peculiarities can so combine with the rest of our constitution as to make us the more useful to our kind, why, then, we should not ·call them in that context points of unhealthiness, but rather the reverse.[37]

"The trouble is that such writers as Nordau use the descriptive names of symptoms merely as an artifice for giving objective authority to their personal dislikes. The medical terms become mere appreciative clubs to knock a man down with. Call a man a cad and you have settled his social status. Call him a degenerate, and you've grouped him with the most loathsome specimens of the race, in spite of the fact that he may be one of its most precious members. The only sort of being, in fact, who can remain as the typical normal man, after all the individuals with degenerative symptoms have been rejected, bust be a perfect nullity. He must, it is true, be able to perform the necessities of nature and adapt himself to his environment so as to come in when it rains; but being free from all the excesses and superfluities that make Man's life interesting, without love, poetry, art, religion, or any other ideal but pride in his non-neurotic constitution, he is the human counterpart of that 'temperance' hotel of which the traveler's handbook said, 'It possesses no other quality to recommend it.' We all remember the sort of schoolboy who used to ask us six times a day to feel his biceps. The sort of man who pounds his mental chest and says to us: See, there isn't a morbid fibre in my composition! is like unto him. Few more profitless members of the race can be found.[38]

"The real lesson of the genius books is that we should welcome sensibilities, impulses, and obsessions if we have them, so long as by their means the field of our experience grows deeper and we contribute the better to the race's stores; that we should broaden our notion of health instead of narrowing it; that we should regard no single element of weakness as fatal—in short, that we should *not be afraid of life*.[39] Rather, all these geniuses and their mental peculiarities are organs by which mankind works out the experience which is its destiny.

"Who shall absolutely say that the morbid has no revelations about the meaning of life? That the healthy minded view so-called is all? A certain tolerance, a certain sympathy, a certain respect, and above all a certain lack of fear, seem to be the best attitude we can carry in our dealing with these regions of human nature. And in thanking you for the attention which you have given to these tedious lectures, let me express a hope that you go away from them with that more positive attitude increased and confirmed."[40]

NOTES

HISTORICAL INTRODUCTION

1. Several summaries of James's activities during this period exist. See Ralph Barton Perry, *The Thought and Character of William James*, vol. II (Boston: Little, Brown, 1935), 155–172; G. W. Allen, *William James: A Biography* (New York: Viking, 1967), 366–388; Grace Foster, "The Psychotherapy of William James," *Psychoanalytic Review*, 32 (July 1943), 300–318; Gardner Murphy and Robert Ballou, *William James on Psychic Research* (New York: Viking, 1960); and H. D. Spoerl, "Abnormal and Social Psychology in the Life of William James," *Journal of Abnormal and Social Psychology*, 37 (January 1942), 3–19. See also H. Ellenberger, *Discovery of the Unconscious* (New York: Basic Books, 1970); Nathan Hale, *Freud and the Americans* (New York: Oxford University Press, 1971); Hale's *James Jackson Putnam and Psychoanalysis* (Cambridge, Mass.: Harvard University Press, 1971), and his *Morton Prince: Psychotherapy and Personality* (Cambridge, Mass.: Harvard University Press, 1975); B. Ross, "William James: A Prime Mover of the Psychoanalytic Movement in America," in G. E. Gifford, ed., *Psychoanalysis, Psychotherapy, and the New England Medical*

Scene, 1894–1944 (New York: Science History Publications, 1978); and finally R. B. Perry's "List of Courses Taught by James in Harvard College." Handwritten MS, James Papers, Houghton Library, Harvard.

2. See Lecture IV: "Multiple Personality."

3. See Hale, *Freud and the Americans*; Gifford ed., *Psychoanalysis, Psychotherapy, and the New England Medical Scene*; and J. C. Burnham, "Psychoanalysis and American Medicine, 1894–1918: Medicine, Science, and Culture," *Psychological Issues Monograph*, 20, vol. V, no. 4.

4. E. Weeks. *The Lowells and Their Institute* (Boston: Little, Brown, 1966).

5. J. E. Pierce, "Janitor's Notebook," in the Lowell Institute Papers, Houghton Library, Harvard.

6. William James to Augustus Lowell, April 18, 1896, in the Lowell Institute Papers, Houghton Library, Harvard.

7. William James to G. H. Howison, April 5, 1897; and James to Howison, July 2, 1897; both in the James Papers, Houghton Library, Harvard.

8. R. B. Perry, handwritten note at the top of page 1 of James's MS lecture notes on Exceptional Mental States, James Papers, Houghton Library, Harvard.

9. See E. Taylor, "The Boston School of Psychotherapy: Science, Healing, and Consciousness in Nineteenth Century New England," Eight Lectures for the Lowell Institute, co-sponsored by the Boston Medical Library, the Massachusetts Medical Society, and the Boston Public Library, where the lectures were held, February–March 1982. Written version in preparation. See also E. Taylor, "William James and C. G. Jung," *Spring: An Annual of Archetypal Psychology and Jungian Thought* (1980), 157–168; E. Taylor, "Louville Eugene Emerson; Psychotherapy, Harvard, and the Early Boston Scene," *Harvard Medical Alumni Bulletin* (1982), 56:2, 42–48; and E. Taylor, "William James on Psychopathology; Reconstruction of the 1896 Lowell Lectures," *Harvard Library Bulletin* (October 1982), 455–479.

10. Henry A. Murray, "Morton Prince: Sketch of his Life and Work," *Harvard Psychological Clinic, 1927–1957* (Cambridge: Harvard University Press, 1957), 5.

LECTURE I: *DREAMS AND HYPNOTISM*

1. See "On 'Dreams and Hypnotism,' " *Boston Transcript,* Oct. 22, 1896; "Dreams and Hypnotism," *Boston Globe,* Oct. 22, 1896; "Professor James's Lectures," *Boston Transcript,* Oct. 31, 1896; "Professor James's Lowell Lectures," *Boston Transcript,* Nov. 17, 1896; and James's letters to Theodore Flournoy, Dec. 7, 1896, Henry James, *The Letters of William James* (Boston: Atlantic Monthly Press, 1920, cited hereafter as *LWJ*), and to George Howison, April 5, 1897, James Papers, Houghton Library, Harvard. James's notes specifically say here "no SPR," meaning no details of work by the Society for Psychical Research on occult themes will be given in the lectures. Instead, he wished to deal with his subject scientifically, from a medical and psychological point of view.

2. St. Paul, religious figure of the New Testament; Cesare Lombroso, late nineteenth-century Italian criminologist; and Immanuel Kant, eighteenth-century German philosopher. Parts of the text here are taken from newspaper accounts; see note 1 above.

3. Professor of psychiatry at Strasbourg, and then at Graz, Krafft-Ebing finally succeeded T. H. Meynert at Vienna and also became president of the Viennese Neurological Society. He was sympathetic to Freud's early work on the sexual etiology of the neurosis, himself taught Alfred Adler, and his theories inspired the young medical intern Carl Gustav Jung.

James had followed Krafft-Ebing's work closely from the 1860s, especially the studies of delirium and melancholia. James's copy of Krafft-Ebing's *Lehrbuch der Psychiatrie* (1888) is copiously marked, and there is some evidence that he used that text in his graduate lectures in mental pathology at

Harvard in both 1893 and 1894. James also made use of
Krafft-Ebing's *Experimentelle Hypnotismus* as soon as the
volume was published in 1893. Harvard Library Charging
Records, Harvard University Archives.

4. R. Krafft-Ebing, *An Experimental Study in the Domain
of Hypnotism,* translated by C. G. Chaddock (New York:
Putnam's Sons, 1889). Neither the English translation nor the
original German edition has been located in the remnants of
James's family library. James did refer to cases of dreams
aggravating hysteria in his review of Santi De Sanctis's *I
Sogni,* etc., in *Psychological Review,* 3 (1896), 681–682. He
also marked the section on dreamy states that aggravated
the symptoms of epileptics in Krafft-Ebing's *Lehrbuch der
Psychiatrie.* See James's copy in Houghton Library, Harvard,
pp. 550–553. Josiah Royce's annotated copy of the case of
Ilma S. is extant in the Widener Library at Harvard.

5. See James's review (unsigned) of B. P. Blood's *Anaesthetic Revelation* in *Atlantic Monthly,* 34 (1874), 627–629;
an account of his experiment with amyl nitrate in Gay
Wilson Allen's *William James: A Biography,* 193; his
references to hashish in the *The Principles of Psychology,* 2
vols. (New York: Henry Holt, 1890), II, 121; the famous
"mescal episode" recounted in *LWJ,* II 37; his article on
"Consciousness under Nitrous Oxide," *Psychological Review,*
5 (1898), 194–196; and see his comments on alcohol, ether,
and chloroform in *Varieties of Religious Experience* (New
York: Longmans, Green, 1902) in the chapter on Mysticism
for drug-related statements on consciousness.

6. Taken from newspaper accounts, note 1 above. Compare
this with *Principles,* II, 294, and *Varieties,* 388.

7. James described this kind of association during dreaming. He recounted Mozart's method of composing, in which
the great musical genius saw the whole of a symphony in a
single glimpse in his mind. "It is a rare feast," he quoted
Mozart as saying. "All the inventing and making goes on in

me as in a beautiful strong dream. But the best of all is the *hearing of it all at once." Principles,* I, 255.

8. In Gay Wilson Allen's *William James: A Biography,* there is recounted a dream of James's in which he saw himself "lecturing in his pajamas," 423; and in 1910, James published an account of a pathological telescoping dream in "A Suggestion about Mysticism," *Journal of Philosophy, Psychology, and Scientific Method,* 7 (1910), 85–92. The account was later analyzed by Erik Erikson in his *Identity, Youth, and Crisis* (New York: Norton, 1968), and provoked a criticism by Saul Rosenzweig, followed by a rejoinder from Erikson. See *Journal of the History of the Behavioral Sciences,* 7 (1970), 258–260.

9. See W. James (unsigned), review on "Moral Medication," *The Nation,* 7 (1868), 50–52; and *Principles,* I, 575–576. In 1897, James reported on an ingenious experiment in which De Sanctis had shown that paranoiacs suffer a greater contraction of the field of vision than normals. See James's review of Santi De Sanctis's *Le Studie dell' Attenzione* in *Psychological Review,* 4 (1897), 659.

10. In a review of Theodore Flournoy's *Des Phénomènes de synopsie* for the *Philosophical Review,* 3 (1894), 88–92, James described the results of experiments by Flournoy and his student Claparède on the evocation of internal imagery by presenting sounds, pictures, or ideas to the subject. The study showed extreme idiosyncrasy of associations for each individual.

11. Compare this with *Principles,* I, 236, and *Varieties,* 197.

12. The chapter on Association in the *Principles* alluded to this phenomenon when James compared the process of association in the normal mind with association in the mind of a genius. The mind of the genius, he said, was more like that of the dreaming state because of the unusual nature of associative currents. When dreaming, the neural paths of irradia-

tion discharge much more spontaneously than in the waking state and are much more capricious, just as they are in the most gifted minds. James commented that "the usual abundance of paths of irradiation seems, in the dormant brain, reduced. A few only are previous, and the most fantastic sequences occur because the currents run—'like sparks in burnt up paper'—wherever the nutrition of the moment creates an opening, but nowhere else."

James Jackson Putnam later used this image of sparks running through burnt-up paper to compare James's dream theory with that of Sigmund Freud, while Mary Whiton Calkins used James's association theory in the interpretation of dream studies done in the psychological laboratory at Wellesley College. See *Principles,* I, 593–594; James Jackson Putnam, "Personal Impressions of Freud and His Work," *Journal of Abnormal Psychology* (December 1909); and Mary Whiton Calkins, "A Statistical Study of Dreams," *American Journal of Psychology,* 5 (1893), 311–329, and her statement in *The History of Psychology in Autobiography,* ed. by Carl Murchinson (Worcester, Mass.: Clark University Press, 1932).

13. *Principles,* I, 593–594; see also George M. Beard, *The Nature and Phenomena of Trance* (New York: Putnam's Sons, 1881), 1.

14. James implied as much in his chapter on Attention in the *Principles* when he said, quoting Sir William Hamilton, "It is reported of Newton that, while engaged in his mathematical researches, he sometimes forgot to dine"—*Principles,* I, 419.

15. Ibid.; James's notes quote p. 304. See also Ralph Barton Perry's *Thought and Character of William James,* I, 246, 260, II, 252; and the review by B. W. Wells in *Encyclopedia Americana,* vol. XVI (New York: American Corp., 1957) of Emile Erckmann and Alexandre Chatrian's *L'Ami Fritz* (Paris: Hachette, 1867).

16. See James's conclusions on the effects of alcohol in his

address to students at Harvard College on Temperance, *Harvard Independent,* June 23, 1881; and his various notes on alcohol, James Papers, Houghton Library, Harvard. See also his statements in *Varieties,* 386.

17. W. Wundt, "Hypnotismus und Suggestion," *Philosophische Studien,* 8 (1892–93), 1–85. James's notes refer to p. 31. In James's copy of this work he has annotated "As in dreams where we see a man [whom we know, but] with a different face." The rest of the article is filled with James's marks and marginal notes, such as "bah!" next to many of Wundt's explanations.

18. Part of the full quotation taken from newspaper accounts, note 1 above.

19. See R. B. Perry's *Thought and Character of William James,* II 188, for one assessment James gave of Janet.

20. See P. Janet, *L'Automatisme psychologique* (Paris: Alcan, 1889), and especially Janet's chapter on Somnambulism in his *Mental State of Hystericals,* translated by C. R. Corson (New York: Putnam's Sons, 1901).

21. T. D. Crothers, *The Trance State in Inebriety: Its Medico-legal Relations,* with an introduction on the nature and character of trance by G. M. Beard, which was read before the New York Medico-Legal Society, Nov. 2, 1881 (Hartford, Conn.: Case, Lockwood & Brainard, 1882). See also list of the most highly prized books and pamphlets in James's library, in the hand of Alice Howe Gibbens James, James Papers, Houghton Library, Harvard. For additional accounts studied by Beard, see his Experiments with the "Jumpers" of Maine, *Popular Science Monthly,* 18 (1881), 170–179. See also Beard's *The Study of Trance, Muscle Reading, and Allied Nervous Phenomena* in *Europe and America,* and *A Defense of Dr. Charcot* (New York, 1882). Copy autographed by WJ, Rare Books, Countway Library of Medicine, Harvard.

22. Crothers, *The Trance State in Inebriety.* James's notes cite pp. 18 and 87(?).

23. Hypnosis was an important experimental tool for James. He had maintained apparatus for conducting experiments on hypnosis with his students at the Harvard Psychological Laboratory; he published at least one statistical study on reaction time in the hypnotic trance, and wrote a widely read summary of hypnotism in the *Principles*; he served as one of the many investigators of the Committee on Hypnotism for the American Society for Psychical Research; and he used hypnosis himself in the treatment of several patients suffering from psychological disturbances whom he took under his care, probably the only patients he ever saw in his career as a medical doctor and practitioner of psychotherapy. See R. S. Harper, "The Laboratory of William James," *Harvard Alumni Bulletin,* 52, Nov. 5, 1949, 169–173; W. James, "Reaction-Time in the Hypnotic Trance," *Proceedings of the American Society for Psychical Research,* 1 (1887), 246–248; chapter 27 in the *Principles*; his report (with G. M. Carnochan) for the Committee on Hypnotism, *Proceedings of the American Society for Psychical Research,* 1 (1886), 95–102; and for his various references to the patients he himself treated, Lecture IV on "Multiple Personality" below.

24. Adapted from original lecture notes plus *Boston Transcript,* Oct. 31, 1896.

25. See also the same point made in *Principles,* II, 59.

26. *Boston Transcript,* Oct. 31, 1896.

27. "If a lot of dots or strokes on a piece of paper be exhibited for a few moments to a person in *normal* condition, with the request that he say how many there are, he will find that they break into groups in his mind's eye, and that whilst he is analyzing and counting one group in his memory the others dissolve. In short, the impression made by the dots changes rapidly into something else. In the trance-subject, on the contrary, it seems to *stick;* I find that persons in the hypnotic state easily count the dots in the mind's eye so long as they do not much exceed twenty in number"—*Principles,* I, 407.

28. James's notes cite only "Hammond's case . . . breaks table," but no such example of Hammond's work has been found. Beard, in his introduction to *The Trance State in Inebriety,* mentions demonstrations he and Hammond gave before the New York Medico-Legal Society around 1877 that involved suggestibility as a function of heightened expectation, but the Society reports do not give details. James used other works by Hammond: *Sleep and Its Derangements* (Philadelphia: Lippincott, 1869) and "A Case of Intellectual Monomania with Mental Depression," *American Journal of Neurology and Psychiatry* (1883), 110–128, WJ's copy with James's note "case of delusions 110," Widener Library. He read Hammond's *Nervous Derangement* along with Wilhelm Griesinger's *Mental Diseases* in preparation for his graduate lectures in mental pathology in 1893, and he used Hammond's *Treatise on Insanity and Its Medical Relations* for the same purpose in 1894 and again in 1896, according to the Library Charging Lists, Harvard Archives.

29. Adapted from Boris Sidis, *The Psychology of Suggestion,* with a preface by William James (New York: Appleton, 1898), 15.

30. James gave a physiological explanation for the mechanism behind hypnagogic imagery in his *Principles,* II, 122ff.

31. We know this because James, in his 1868 review of Liébeault's *Du Sommeil et des états analogues* for *The Nation,* had already pointed out that in ordinary sleep, "the tactile sensibility being the last to expire . . . it is often possible, by placing the fingers for a couple of minutes on the forehead or another part of the skin of the sleeper, to lead out the attention, as it were, through the fingers to the voice, and thence to various subjects which one might suggest." See W. James (unsigned), review on "Moral Medication," *The Nation,* 7 (1868), 50–52.

32. James's notes on "Sleep-Trance" contain an English translation of Maury's famous examples of dream productions from external stimulation.

33. L. F. A. Maury, *Le Sommeil et les rêves* (Paris: Didier, 1864); see also James's annotated copy of Maury's article on suggestion during sleep in *Revue de l'hypnotisme*, 12 (1898), Countway Library of Medicine, Lydiard Horton Collection, Harvard; and W. R. Newbold, "Subconscious Reasoning," *Proceedings of the English Society for Psychical Research,* 12 (June 1896), 19, for this example in James's notes. James also cited the work of Maury in Notebook 26, an Index Rerum he kept over the years with bibliographic resources for his various literary projects, James Papers, Houghton Library, Harvard.

34. In P. Tissié's *Les Rêves, phsiologie et pathologie* (Paris: Alcan, 1890), 8.

35. James Mark Baldwin, "Dream Excitation," *Science* (1880), in James's folder on "Sleep-Trance," James Papers, Houghton Library, Harvard.

36. Ibid., 164; courtesy of Oscar Zumbrano.

37. Ibid., 102.

38. Ibid., 103.

39. *Principles,* I, 213; and James's review of Liébeault, note 31 above. In his chapter on Hypnotism, James cites the important work of J. K. Mitchell, "On Animal Magnetism, or Vital Induction," in *Five Essays,* ed. by S. W. Mitchell (Philadelphia: Lippincott, 1859), 143–273.

40. For Delboeuf's influence on James, see Perry's *Thought and Character of William James,* II, 775. We know that James was present at the International Congress of Experimental Psychology held in Paris, Aug. 6–10, 1889, when Delboeuf reported on some of his experiments in post-hypnotic suggestion. See *Proceedings of the English Society for Psychical Research,* 6 (1889–90), 182. See also James's references in *Principles,* II, 612.

41. See *Proceedings of the English Society for Psychical Research,* 12 (1896–97), 36, although James could have been referring to Thomson J. Hudson's *Law of Psychic Phenomena* (Chicago: McClurg, 1893), especially chapter 13.

42. Found in James's "Notes on Psychical Research," Houghton Library, Harvard.

43. H. Bernheim, "De l'amaurose hystérique et de l'amaurose suggestion," *Revue de l'hypnotisme*, 3 (1889), 68–70; and "De influence hypnotique et de ses divers degrés," ibid., 230–231, for James's annotations, Rare Books, Countway Library of Medicine, Lydiard Horton Collection, Harvard. The "page 220" reference has not been located.

44. Cited in F. W. H. Myers, "The Subliminal Consciousness," *Proceedings of the English Society for Psychical Research*, 8 (1892), 375; see P. Tissié, *Les Aliénés voyageurs* (Paris: Octave Doin, 1887), for additional examples.

LECTURE II: *AUTOMATISM*

1. "Power of Hypnotic Influence; Second Lecture in Lowell Institute Course by Professor James on Mental States," *Boston Sunday Herald*, Oct. 25, 1896, 3.

2. Taken from extra set of lecture notes on "Hysteria and Hypnosis," James Papers, Houghton Library, Harvard.

3. Charles Féré and George Hermann Meyer. Féré had coauthored *Animal Magnetism* with Alfred Binet, and had published other well-known researches, among them his 1899 work on *The Sexual Instinct: Evolution and Dissolution*. James had review Féré's *La Pathologie des emotions* in the *Philosophical Review* for 1893. The discussion of Meyer and Féré on the negative after-image James first elaborated upon in his chapter on Imagination in the *Principles*, II, 66–68.

4. James cited Bernheim's experiments on auditory deafness in the chapter on Hypnotism in the *Principles*, and reviewed instances of systematized visual blindness in his notice of Bernheim's "Psychical Nature of Hysterical Unilateral Amblyopia" in the *Psychological Review*, 1 (1894), 93–94. James's copy of Bernheim's *Hypnotisme* (Paris: Octave Doin, 1891)

was sold at a Harvard College Library booksale for 50¢.
James's penciled index in this volume refers to the discussion
of auditory deafness under hypnosis, 130–136.

5. In addition to being a close friend of James's, Edmund
Gurney was a founder and secretary of the English Society
for Psychical Research. He published pioneering experiments
on the effects of hypnotism and was the principal author, with
F. W. H. Myers and Frank Podmore, of *Phantasms of the
Living,* which James reviewed for *Science* in 1887. By 1888,
Gurney was dead from an overdose of chloral hydrate—"one
of life's stupidest tragedies," James had written to his brother
Henry, *LWJ,* I, 279–280.

6. Taken from extra set of lecture notes on "Hysteria and
Hypnosis."

7. Moll's early work on hypnotism was well known to
James, who had copiously marked Moll's original 1889
German edition of *Der Hypnotismus.* James later made some
notes in an English translation of the same work. See A. Moll,
Hypnotism (New York: Scribners, 1892), p. 143; also James's
copy of Moll's *Der Hypnotismus* (Berlin: Fischer, 1889), and
his *Der Rapport der Hypnose* (Leipzig: Verlag Abel, 1892),
Houghton Library, Harvard, for James's annotations. See also
note 1 above.

8. J. Liègeois, "Suggestion hypnotique dans ses rapports
avec le droit civil et le droit criminal," *Revue de l'hypnotisme,* 1 (1887), 148–150, WJ's copy, Lydiard Horton Collection, Rare Books, Countway Library of Medicine, Harvard. James's reference to "p. 34" has not been located.

9. E. Gurney, "Some Peculiarities of the Post-Hypnotic
Trance," *Proceedings of the English Society for Psychical
Research,* 4 (1886–87), 290–192.

10. Ibid., 296.

11. W. James, Notice of A. H. Pierce's *Subliminal Self,* F.
Podmore's *Reply,* A. von Schrenck-Notzing's *Uber Spaltung
der Persönlichkeit,* and S. Landmann's *Die Mehrheit Geistiger
Persönlichkeiten,* in the *Psychological Review,* 3 (1896), 682–

684. See also list of the most highly prized books and pamphlets in James's library, in the hand of Alice Howe Gibbens James, James Papers, Houghton Library, Harvard.

12. P. Janet, "Les Actes inconscients et le dédoublement de la personnalité pendant le somnambulisme provoqué, *Revue philosophique*, 22 (1886); James's notes cite pp. 585–586. James extensively annotated Janet's *L'Automatisme psychologique* (1889), which contains most of the material from essays Janet published throughout the late 1880s. Nevertheless, in his Exceptional Mental States Lectures, James almost always refers to these earlier articles. See also James's "The Hidden Self," *Scribner's Magazine*, 7 (1890), 361–373.

13. Myers and the English group had in fact embraced James as a colleague and friend in 1882, whereupon James inaugurated the American branch of the English Society on his return to Harvard in 1884, with Josiah Royce, G. Stanley Hall, Henry Pickering Bowditch, J. J. Putnam, Simon Newcomb, Phillips Brooks, and Asa Gray, among others, as charter members.

Myers and James had exchanged frequent letters and visits over the years, and it appears that James's great attraction to Myers's work lay not in psychic phenomena themselves but rather in Myers's emphasis on growth-oriented aspects of the subconscious. James had always hoped that Myers would complete the great work on subliminal consciousness, but like Charles Sanders Peirce's long-anticipated works on logic, Myers's magnum opus was never completed. Instead, Myers's widow, with the help of others, tried to complete the project by bringing out *Human Personality and Its Survival of Bodily Death* posthumously in 1903, which James reviewed sympathetically. Myers's many essays entitled "Subliminal Consciousness" in the English Society's *Journal* and *Proceedings* remain, however, his clearest and most provocative statements. See James's review of Myers's contribution to Gurney and Podmore's *Phantasms of the Living* in *Science*, 9 (1887), 18–20; James's review of Myers's *Science and a Future Life* in *The Nation,* 57 (1893), 176–177; James's eulogy on "Frederick Myers's Services to Psychology," *Proceedings of the English Society for Psychical Research,* 17 (1901), 13–23; and his posthumous review of Myers's *Human Personality* in *Proceedings of the English Society for Psychical Research,* 18 (1903), 22–33.

14. Myers, "The Subliminal Consciousness," *Proceedings of the English Society for Psychical Research,* 7 (1891–92), 301–302.

15. Ibid., 306.

16. James's notes cite Thomas Barkworth, "Duplex Personality," *Proceedings of the English Society for Psychical Research,* 6 (1889–90), 86.

17. See James's marked copy of Max Dessoir's *Das Dopple Ich* (Leipzig: E. Günther, 1890), Houghton Library, Harvard; and Dessoir's presentation copy to James of *Experimentelle Pathopsychologie,* 59–106, extracted from a larger work, Houghton Library, Harvard. Both annotated.

18. James on Miss X's Crystal Vision, in "What Psychical Research Has Accomplished," *The Will to Believe and Other Essays in Philosophy* (New York: Longmans, Green, 1897), 314–315.

19. Lang had also written numerous accounts of various psychic events and was interested in the entire range of possibilities presented by the hypothesis of a superior secondary intelligence. James had copies of both *Cock Lane and Common Sense* and *The Making of Religion* in his family library. See List of Books Presented to Harvard College from the Library of William James, 1923, Widener Library Reference Room, Harvard.

20. W. James, Notice of Andrew Lang's *Cock Lane and Common Sense,* and of C. Du Prel's *Die Entdeckung der Seele durch die Geheimwissenschaften,* in *Psychological Review,* 1 (1894), 630–632.

21. Taken from the *Journal of the English Society for Psychical Research* (June 1895), 101–102.

22. See, for instance, Prince's "Some of the Revelations of Hypnotism" in *Boston Medical and Surgical Journal,* May 8, 1890, 475–476, and Records of the Boston Medico-Legal Society, Rare Books, Countway Library of Medicine, Harvard; also Prince's *Clinical and Experimental Studies in Personality,* ed. by A. A. Roback (Cambridge, Mass.: Sci-Art Publishers, 1929), for a wide selection of Prince's articles similar to James's own interests in psychopathology.

23. See M. Prince, "Contribution to the Study of Hysteria and Hypnosis," delivered at the 1891 meeting of the American Neurological Association, and published in the *Proceedings of the English Society for Psychical Research,* 14 (1899), 79–97.

24. See W. James (unsigned), Notice of E. Sargent's *Planchette: or the Despair of Science* in the *Boston Daily Advertiser,* March 10, 1896; W. James, "Notes on Automatic Writing," *Proceedings of the American Society for Psychical Research,* 1 (1889), 548–564; *Principles,* I, 393ff.; and James's Address of the President, *Proceedings of the English Society for Psychical Research,* 12 (1896), 2–10. For James's influence on Gertrude Stein and the training she received in automatic writing in the Harvard Psychological Laboratory, see M. J. Hoffman, "Gertrude Stein and the Psychological Laboratory," *American Quarterly,* 17: 1 (Spring 1965), 127–132; M. J. Hoffman, "Gertrude Stein and William James," *The Personalist,* 47 (April 1966), 226–233; D. Gallup, ed., *The Flowers of Friendship: Letters Written to Gertrude Stein* (New York: Knopf, 1953); G. Stein, "Normal Motor Automatism," *Psychological Review,* 3 (1896), 492–512 (with Leon Solomons); G. Stein, "Cultivated Motor Automatism," *Psychological Review,* 5 (1898), 295–306; and Myers's review in *Proceedings of the English Society for Psychical Research,* 12 (1896–97), 316. For other James contributions, see his "A Case of Psychic Automatism, Including 'Speaking in Tongues,'" *Proceedings of the English Society for Psychical Research,* 12 (1896), 277–279; *Varieties,* pp. 62,

478; "A Case of Automatic Drawing," *Popular Science Monthly* 78 (1904), 175–176; and the "Report on Mrs. Piper's Hodgson Control," *Proceedings of the American Society for Psychical Research*, 3 (1909), 470–589.

25. Helen R. Albee, *The Gleam* (New York: Henry Holt, 1911), pp. 74–75.

26. Myers, "The Subliminal Consciousness," *Proceedings of the English Society for Psychical Research*, 90 (1893–94), 109–112; see also James's copy of Mrs. Underwood's *Automatic or Spirit Writing with Other Psychic Experiences* (Chicago: Thomas & Newman, 1896), Widener Library, Harvard.

27. James's "Notes on Automatic Writing," *Proceedings of the American Society for Psychical Research*, 1 (1889), 556; see also *Principles*, I, 394–396.

28. See *Varieties*, 13, 418, and 478, for references to St. Paul's visions, ecstasies, and the gift of tongues.

29. *Boston Sunday Herald*, Oct. 25, 1896, 3.

LECTURE III: *HYSTERIA*

1. For a general overview of James's lecture on "Hysteria," see "Prof. James on Exceptional Mental States," *Boston Transcript*, Oct. 29, 1896, 6.

2. Newbold, in particular, was a correspondent and former student of James's, and throughout 1896 had published a series of articles parallel to the topics of the Exceptional Mental States Lectures in the *Popular Science Monthly*. There he quoted James, sympathetically reviewed the work of Janet, Gurney, Binet, and others, and supported Myers's formulation of an intelligent subliminal life. See H. Nichols, "The Motor Power of Ideas," *Philosophical Review*, 4 (1895), 174–185; W. R. Newbold, "Experimental Induction of Automatic Processes," *Psychological Review*, 2 (1895), 348–362; and Newbold's essays on "Suggestibility, Automatism, and Kindred Phenomena," "Normal and Heightened Suggesti-

bility," "The Hypnotic State, Trance, Ecstasy," "Post-Hypnotic and Criminal Suggestion," and so on in consecutive issues of *Popular Science Monthly,* beginning January 1896, especially XLIX, 4, 516, for references to James.

3. *Principles,* I, 202–203.

4. Ibid., 203; see also James's "The Hidden Self," op. cit., 361–373.

5. See also *Principles,* I, 386.

6. James had read Charcot's early works on neurology and had traveled to Paris in 1882 to attend his lectures. He kept in close touch with Charcot's studies through Delboeuf, Janet, and various American visitors such as Morton Prince; he cited Charcot extensively in the *Principles* in 1890 and had referred to the new edition of Charcot's complete works when preparing for the graduate lectures in mental pathology at Harvard as late as 1893. See Perry, *Thought and Character of William James,* II, 5; *Principles,* I, 54–55, II, 58, 596; and the Harvard University Charging Records, March 23, 1892.

7. See extra set of Houghton notes containing partial contents of this lecture, labeled "Hypnosis-Hysteria."

8. See James's copy of Janet's *L'Automatisme psychologique,* p. 291, and James's pencilled index note in the back for this case of "elective anaesthesia," Houghton Library, Harvard.

9. Ibid., 287.

10. See Myers's "Subliminal Consciousness," *Proceedings of the English Society for Psychical Research,* 7 (1891–92), 302, and 9 (1893–94), 5. James very clearly emphasized in the *Varieties* that healthy, growth-oriented ideas could be suggested just as easily as sick ones. See his chapter on Conversion.

11. See James's copy of Janet's *L'Automatisme psychologique,* 295.

Binet probably first met James in 1889 at the International Congress of Experimental Psychology in Paris. They had a number of friends in common; both cited each other's work extensively, and we know that James had followed Binet's

articles in the *Revue philosophique.* James referred to Binet's
La Psychologie du raisonnement in the *Principles;* he used
Binet's *Le Magnétisme animal, La possession de F.*
Fontaine, Les Altérations de la personnalité, and the English translation
of *The Psychic Life of Micro-organisms* in his graduate lec-
tures in mental pathology at Harvard; and he annotated
copies of Binet's *Les Altérations, L'Ame et le corps,* and
Psychologie des grands calculateurs.

12. *Principles,* I, 203ff., II, 71, 74, 128ff., 130, 167, 491, and
520; Harvard College Library Charging Records, 1889, 1891,
1893–94; WJ's copy of Binet's *Les Altérations de la personnalité* (Paris: Alcan, 1892) with James's notes and Binet's
inscription to James, Houghton Library, Harvard. For more
on James's interest in Binet, see Binet's *L'Ame et le corps*
(1905) with James's notes, Houghton Library, Harvard, and
"Report to the Committee on Hypnotism," *Proceedings of
the American Society for Psychical Research,* 1 (1886), 97f.

13. Binet's *Altérations;* James's note cites p. 125, note 12.
A reference to "Krieger" in James's 1896 notes has not been
identified.

14. Ibid., 108.

15. Ibid., 120.

16. Ibid., 184–187, 190.

17. *Principles,* I, 206–207, as well as Janet's *L'Automatisme
psychologique;* see James's copy with penciled index note "p.
276–277," Houghton Library, Harvard. See also James's "The
Hidden Self," op cit.

18. *Principles,* I, 203f. The following summary of Binet's
comments on childhood automatisms is abstracted from the
English translation of his article in R. H. Pollack and M. W.
Brenner, eds., *The Experimental Psychology of Alfred Binet:
Selected Papers* (New York: Springer, 1969), 161–164. A
reference to "Adamson" in James's 1896 notes has not been
identified.

19. See W. James, Notice of C. Wernicke's *Grundriss der
Psychiatrie* in *Psychological Review,* 4 (1897), 194, for James's

comparison of Janet and Breuer and Freud. See also W. James, Notice of P. Janet's *Etat mental des hystériques,* and *L'Amnésie continue,* J. Breuer and S. Freud's *Uber den Psychischen Mechanismus Hysterischer Phänomene,* and L. E. Whipple's *Philosophy of Mental Healing,* all in *Psychological Review,* 1 (1894), 195–200. For a different interpretation, see Hale, *Freud and the Americans,* p. 183; B. Ross, "William James: A Prime Mover of the Psychoanalytic Movement in America," G. E. Gifford, ed., *Psychoanalysis, Psychotherapy, and the New England Medical Scene, 1894–1944,* 10–23; and J. Gach, "Culture and Complex: On the Early History of Psychoanalysis in America," in E. R. Wallace and L. C. Pressley, eds., *Essays in the History of Psychiatry* (Columbia, S.C.: Hall Psychiatric Institute, 1980), 137. For a similar comparison in *Varieties,* see pp. 234–235. Also James's unmarked copy of L. E. Whipple's *Philosophy and Mental Healing, A Practical Exposition of Natural Restorative Power* (New York: Metaphysical Publishing Co., 1893), Widener Library, Harvard.

20. James on Janet (1894), 194–195 (see note 19 above).

21. Ibid., 199.

22. Ibid., 196.

23. Ibid., 199.

24. See James's review of Janet's "Histoire d'une Idée Fixe" in *Psychological Review,* 1 (1894), 316.

25. Ibid.

26. Janet's *Etat mental des hystériques,* 375 (English tr.).

27. James's review of Janet's *Etat mental des hystériques,* 198.

28. James, "The Hidden Self," op cit., 372–373.

29. Adapted from Freud's case of Miss Lucy R.; see James's copy of *Studien über Hysterie* (Leipzig and Vienna: Franz Deuticke, 1895), Houghton Library, Harvard.

30. This was the final quotation that James used on an alternate set of lecture notes marked "Hypnosis-Hysteria," James Papers, Houghton Library, Harvard.

LECTURE IV: *MULTIPLE PERSONALITY*

1. *Principles,* I, 375ff.; see also "Peculiar Mental States: Distinct Orders of Double Personality Described," *Boston Sunday Herald,* Nov. 1, 1896, 22.

2. The case of Albert is outlined in greatest detail in Tissié's *Les Aliénés voyageurs* (Paris: Octave Doin, 1887).

3. See F. Raymond and P. Janet, "Les Délires ambulatoires ou les fugues," *Gazette des Hôpitaux* (1895), 754–762; and F. Raymond, *Maladies du système nerveux* (Paris: Octave Doin, 1896), 592–637.

4. See Allen, *William James: A Biography,* p. 312, for reference to James's treatment of a few patients in his home in 1889, one quite successfully. James's letters to his wife concerning the case of Ansel Bourne suggest a therapeutic approach that James took in trying to restore Bourne's lost memories; and James's letter to Henry William Rankin describes patients "worked on" by faith healers at James's request—James to Rankin, June 12, 1897, Hocking Papers, Houghton Library, Harvard, by permission. For the best written account yet produced on William's sister, see J. Strause, *Alice James: A Biography* (Boston: Houghton Mifflin, 1980).

5. See Ernest Earnest, *S. Weir Mitchell: Novelist and Physician* (Philadelphia: University of Pennsylvania Press, 1950), and Anna Robeson Burr, *Weir Mitchell: His Life and Letters* (New York: Duffield, 1930), for the relationship between Mitchell and James.

6. Taken from *Principles,* I, 381–382. See also James's presentation copy from Silas Weir Mitchell, "Mary Reynolds: A Case of Double Consciousness," *Transactions of the College of Physicians and Surgeons,* Philadelphia, April 4, 1888, Houghton Library, Harvard; and the list of the most highly prized books and pamphlets in James's library, done in the hand of Alice Howe Gibbens James, James Papers, Houghton Library, Harvard.

7. Taken from *Principles,* I, 391–392; and Richard Hodgson's account in the *Proceedings of the English Society for Psychical Research,* 7 (1891). See also James's copy of *The Wonderful Work of God: The Case of Ansel Bourne* (Fall River, Mass., 1877), Houghton Library, Harvard, listed on his most highly prized list. And see Morton Prince to Henry James, Jr., 1920, James Papers, Houghton Library, Harvard.

8. The following is taken from James's copy of A. H. Dailey's *Mollie Fancher. "Who Am I?" An Enigma,* which contains James's signature and address, marginal markings, pencilled index on the back flyleaf, in addition to two letters inserted in the pages. One was from Mollie Fancher to James dated April 3, 1895, which shows that James had met Mollie and previously written a letter to her. The other was from Pierre Janet to James, dated June 8, 1895, in which Janet comments on the Fancher case—Rare Books, Countway Library of Medicine, Harvard. See also A. A. Walsh, "Mollie Fancher: The Brooklyn Enigma," *New Port Magazine* (Salve Regina College), 1 (1978), 2; and *Proceedings of the English Society for Psychical Research,* 14 (1899), 396.

9. Ibid.

10. W. James, "Hysteria, Alternating Personality, Paramnesia, and Thought Transference," Notice of R. Osgood Mason's "Duplex Personality, etc.," in the *Psychological Review,* 1 (1894), 316.

11. *Principles,* I, 380; see also Tucker's translation of Azam's original article in the *Journal of Nervous and Mental Disease* (October 1878).

12. From James's "The Hidden Self," op. cit., 366–367. I have altered the punctuation slightly here in order to simplify the problem of Janet, James, and myself quoting Leonie simultaneously.

13. *Principles,* I, 210.

14. See *Principles,* I, 227–228. James's notes cite P. Janet, "Actes inconscients, etc.," *Revue philosophique,* 22 (1886), 589.

15. F. W. H. Myers, "French Experiments on the Strata of Personality," *Proceedings of the English Society for Psychical Research,* 5 (1888–89), 387.

16. *Principles,* I, 393.

17. J. W. Cadwell, *The "Delusion" of Spiritualism Compared with a Belief in the Bible* (Meriden, Conn., 1884), WJ's copy, Widener Library, Harvard.

18. Ibid., 25.

19. *Principles,* I, 397–398: See also James's own copy of *Lurancy Venum: The Watseka Wonder,* Houghton Library, Harvard.

20. Myers, "French Experiments on the Strata of Personality," op. cit., 374–397, esp. 387; and Myers's "Multiplex Personality," *Proceedings of the English Society for Psychical Research,* 4 (1886–87), 496–514.

21. The following paragraphs are taken directly from the original 1896 lecture notes.

22. This undoubtedly refers to the family of Henry Nottidge Moseley, the English naturalist, and his father, the distinguished mathematician. Both generations of Moseleys had established rigorous criteria for validating scientific observations in their respective fields. Both were well known for their inborn aversion to accepting any statement or recorded observation they had not been able to verify for themselves. The younger Moseley was probably an acquaintance of C. S. Peirce. See *Dictionary of National Biography,* XXXIX, 1894 edn., pp. 175–177.

23. For additional statements on the relation of heterogeneous personalities to religious genius, see *Varieties,* 242; also James's chapter on the Divided Self and Its Process of Unification. There is more on the receptivity of the subliminal, particularly on the subconscious incubation that takes place during religious conversion, in his chapter on Conversion; on the mechanism of catharsis as well as religious transformation in his chapter on Saintliness; and additional

comments on subconscious invasions in his concluding chapter.

LECTURE V: *DEMONIACAL POSSESSION*

1. See *Boston Transcript*, Nov. 5, 1896; W. James, Review of Nevius's *Demon Possession and Allied Themes* in *The Nation*, Aug. 22, 1895, 139; and James's review of Nevius in the *Psychological Review*, 2 (September 1895), 529–531.

2. See Bernard Sachs's account of James's lecture on "Demoniacal Possession" in "Reports of the New York Neurological Society," published in the *Boston Medical and Surgical Journal*, March 4, 1897, 210–212, and the *Journal of Nervous and Mental Disease* (May 1897), 279–282. In a biographical statement, Sachs said that "psychology under William James had a determining influence on my career"—see *Barney Sachs, 1858–1944* (New York: Privately printed, 1949), 32; also Haymaker's *Founders of Modern Neurology* (New York: Thomas, 1970), 513; and Minutes of the New York Neurological Society for Feb. 2, 1897, Courtesy of Mrs. Alice D. Weaver, Archivist, Malloch Rare Book and History Room, New York Academy of Medicine, by permission of Dr. Eugene S. Flamm, secretary of the New York Neurological Society.

3. R. C. Caldwell, "Demonolatry, Devil-Dancing, and Demoniacal Possession," *Contemporary Review*, 27 (1876), 369–376 (WJ's annotations). The complete set of early issues in Widener Library belonged to WJ and was given to Harvard by the James Estate. See issues for other articles containing WJ's annotations.

4. Sachs transcribed this idea of a "sunny land" incorrectly. What James had said was "summer land," a term common in spiritualist circles and used by Myers to refer to the optimistic descriptions of life after death alleged by various psychic mediums. See *Principles*, II, 228.

5. See F. Greenslet, *The Lowells and Their Seven Worlds* (Boston: Houghton Mifflin, 1946).

6. P. Lowell, *Occult Japan or the Way of the Gods: An Esoteric Study of Japanese Personality and Possession* (Boston: Houghton Mifflin, 1894), WJ's annotated copy, Houghton Library, Harvard. James's notes cite "Ontaké, Percival Lowell, 153."

7. On his return to the United States, Nevius turned the unpublished work over to Henry William Rankin, the Reverend Rankin's son, asking him to add a bibliography and see the work through the press. Nevius then returned to China and died soon afterwards.

Rankin, true to his word, added a 100-page bibliography and had the book published in 1895 through Fleming Revel & Company. He immediately sent James three copies. In his accompanying letter, Rankin asked James for a review of the book and offered any of the volumes in the bibliography for James's own use. James took Rankin up on the offer and reviewed the book in *The Nation* and the *Psychological Review*. He kept one copy of the book, which he marked up, and gave the other two to the Harvard College Library.

James began to receive books from Rankin almost immediately, books that he subsequently used in preparing for the Demon Possession lecture. Several years later, Rankin sent James some much-needed books on religious themes, especially spiritual biographies, which James incorporated into the *Varieties of Religious Experience* (Rankin was cited in the preface as an important contributor). Their correspondence lasted about twelve years, Rankin writing long theological tracts to James on Presbyterian missionary Christianity, James always responding with a brief letter or a postcard. After James's death, Rankin supplied Henry James, Jr., with the correspondence in preparation for the two-volume *Letters of William James* (1920). Henry Jr. kept the letters nearly ten years because World War I intervened, preventing him from finishing the project. In 1932 Rankin offered the letters to William Ernest Hocking, then chairman of the Philosophy Department at Harvard. The letters from James to Rankin are still among the Hocking Papers at Harvard. In addition, Rankin's biographical file in the Harvard Archives reveals that, unknown to James, Rankin had been a student of his in the first courses James taught on anatomy and physiology at Harvard in 1872. Rankin had lasted only six weeks, however; he dropped out because of ill health. See J. L. Nevius, *Demon Possession and Allied Themes* (New York: Fleming Revel, 1895), 104, WJ's annotated copy, given as a gift to James by Henry William Rankin.

8. Nevius, ibid., 106–107.

9. Caldwell, "Demonolatry, Devil-Dancing, and Demoniacal Possession," op. cit., 374–376, WJ's annotated and underlined copy, Widener Library, Harvard. See also Houghton notes, 31, for original reference.

10. James's review of Nevius's *Demon Possession and Allied Themes* in the *Psychological Review*, 2 (September 1895), 529–531.

11. Verbatim from Sach's account of the lecture, note 2 above.

12. Henri Boguet, *Discours des sorciers, avec six advis en faict de sorcelerie, et une instruction pour un guje en semblable matière* (Lyon, 2nd edn., 1603), 1. Courtesy of Bernadette Perrault.

13. D. Hack-Tuke, *A Dictionary of Psychological Medicine* (Philadelphia: Blakiston, 1892), 213.

14. References to Mitchell's work on imitative chorea appear in *The American Journal of Medical Sciences*, 58 (1889), 178–179.

15. James marked up the Harvard College Library copy of Constans's *Relation sur une epidémie d'hystéro-démonopathie* extensively during the 1890s; his reading of the book has been confirmed by numerous entries in the Harvard College Library Charging Records. James's notes cite page "23 plus," and the marginal marks scattered throughout the book

suggest that he may have scanned the pages while he talked to his audience, summarizing as he went along. The account was as Sachs described it, but the details are important for James's conclusion to this lecture, and for cross reference with details of another epidemic James used to open his next lecture, "Witchcraft." See A. Constans, *Hystéro-démonopathie en 1861* (Paris: Adrien Delahaye, 1863), WJ's annotations in James Walker's copy, Widener Library, Harvard.

16. Ibid., page "23 plus."

17. James had cited this work in the *Principles* and borrowed the volume from the Harvard College Library several times in preparing for his graduate lectures in mental pathology during the 1890s. The Harvard College Library copy contains characteristic marginal marks, and his 1896 lecture notes cite "page 93," which, judging by the pencilled instructions in the margin, he read out to the audience. See Giuseppe Chiap and Fernando Franzolini, *L'Epidemia di Istero-Demonopathie in Verzegniss* (Reggio Nell' Emilia, 1879). See WJ's annotations in Houghton Library, Harvard.

18. Ibid., 93.

19. Gabriel Jogand-Pages and "Dr. Bataille," *Le Diable au XIXe siècle* (Paris: Delhomme et Briguet, 1893–94), vol. 1, 930. See also Henry Lea's exposé of Taxil in *Lippincott's Magazine*, 1900.

20. James to Rankin, Feb. 1, 1897, Hocking Papers, Houghton Library, Harvard. See also *LWJ*, II, 55.

21. B. Sachs, note 2 above. Of this group of New York neurologists, Charles Loomis Dana and Mary Putnam Jacobi were the most well known. Dana had been a friend and assistant to George Miller Beard; he taught practical psychotherapy at Cornell Medical College, and wrote extensively on the relationship between psychology and psychiatry. Dana believed that psychoanalysis had only limited application with certain kinds of patients.

Mary Putnam Jacobi was a medical pioneer in the late nineteenth century. Trained in Europe, her knowledge and skill surpassed that of most of her male colleagues, who only grudgingly accepted her into a male profession. Daughter of the well-known New York book publisher, she was also known as an essayist and reformer in the field of medical education.

Barrett Wendell delivered his lecture, "Were the Salem Witches Guiltless?" before the Essex Institute on Feb. 29, 1892, in Salem, Massachusetts. Sachs did not cite this title correctly in the published discussion. Also, the other participants have not been identified.

LECTURE VI: *WITCHCRAFT*

1. James's notes say, "Recap. Accusations of Rollande, of Joan Berger, of Herz (by Zilk)," referring in part to Lecture V, "Demoniacal Possession." See also W. G. Soldan on modern instances of witchcraft, quoted in Snell, with James's marginal marks, p. 60, note 9 below.

2. See Boris Sidis, *Psychology of Suggestion,* with preface by William James (New York: Appleton, 1898), 323.

3. Ibid., 326–327.

4. Ibid., 320.

5. See *Boston Transcript,* Nov. 17, 1896; Courtesy of Professor James Anderson, Williams College, and Harvard Archives.

6. James, "Is Life Worth Living?" in *The Will to Believe,* 47–48.

7. See C. K. Sharpe, *Historical Account of Witchcraft in Scotland* (London, 1884), which James had read.

8. The Harvard Library Charging Records show that James checked out a copy of the *Malleus* that came from the old Gore Hall Library collection. The alcove number in the Charging Records is 17½.119.8. A search of all extant copies

of the *Malleus* at Harvard revealed that the copy James used is now in the Houghton Library, catalogued under a new call number, 24244.13 (1620–21 edn.). The old Gore Hall Library number is still in the book, now crossed out, and on the last blank page there appears a brief penciled index in James's handwriting. See J. Sprenger, *Malleus Maleficarum*, Lugduni, Sumptibus Claudi, Landry, 1620–21, Harvard Library Charging Records, Harvard Archives. The copy of the *Malleus* used in this reconstruction is Montague Summers's translation (London: Pushkin Press, 1948).

9. The Harvard College Library copy of Snell's work, probably purchased at James's request in 1892, contains James's marginal marks and a short pencilled index on the last two blank pages. According to the Charging Records, James withdrew the book from the library in preparation for his graduate lectures in mental pathology several times during the 1890s. This is corroborated by the library stamp on the inside back cover, which contains dates beginning in 1893, renewed twice in 1895, and due again in November of 1896, the month this lecture was first given. See Otto Snell, *Hexenprozesse und Geistesstörung: Psychiatrische Untersuchungen* (Munich: Verlag von J. F. Lehmann, 1891). Widener Library #24244.34 was given to the library from the bequest of James Walker on March 3, 1892. The book has not been checked out of the library since James returned it, except to be included in the present bibliography.

10. Ibid., 23.

11. Summers's translation of the *Malleus*, vii–x.

12. Ibid., 215.

13. Ibid., 228.

14. Ibid., 226.

15. For the case of Anna Eve, James's notes cite "Baissac, 670," meaning Jules Baissac's *Les Grands jours de la sorcellerie*. The Harvard College Library copy of this work in the original French edition (Paris: Librairie C. Klincksieck, 1890) contains James's characteristic marginal marks, and a

half-dozen page references on the last blank page of the book, where James usually entered his own pencilled index. The pencilled index refers to page 670, where James's marks appear in the margins, and to page 673, concerning the case of Anna Eve. James's index refers also to page 592, where details of the case of John Junius are given. Similarly, on page 541, James's marginal marks appear next to the well-known list of questions put before the Montpellier Faculty of Medicine. According to the Charging Lists, James may have kept this volume out of the library from 1894 through 1896.

His lecture notes also cite Wilhelm Gottlieb Soldan's *Geschichte der Hexenprozesse* (Stuttgart: J. C. Cotta, 1843), vol. II, in reference to the cases of Anna Eve and John Junius. James checked this work out during the spring of 1894, and probably again for the lectures in 1896. See Library Charging Lists, Harvard Archives.

16. Baissac, *Les Grands jours de la sorcellerie.* James also cites "Soldan II," which refers to Soldan's *Geschichte der Hexenprozesse,* II.

17. James's notes cite Baissac, pp. 529, 125–128.

18. James had addressed this problem of objective certitude in an essay from *The Will to Believe.* There he said that no proposition has ever existed except where someone has thought of it as absolutely true, while his neighbor deemed it absolutely false. Neither of these absolutists seems to have considered that the trouble may all the time lie in the certainty invested in the proposition, for "the intellect even with truth directly within its grasp, may have no infallible signal for knowing whether it be true or no. When, indeed, one remembers that the most striking practical application of life to the doctrine of objective certitude has been the conscientious labors of the Holy Office of the Inquisition, one feels less tempted than ever to lend the doctrine a respectful ear"—James, "The Sentiment of Rationality," in *The Will to Believe,* 16–17.

19. William Edward Hartpole Lecky, *History of the Rise*

and Influence of the Spirit of Rationalism in Europe, 2 vols. (New York: Appleton, 1865), I, 137–138.

20. For Calmeil's view, see his *De la folie: considérée sous le point de vue pathologique, philosophique, historique et judiciaire* (Paris: Baillière, 1845), Widener copy (vol. 1), which contains James's extensive hand-pencilled index on the last blank page and marginal markings throughout. For James's interpretation of Michelet, see *Boston Transcript,* Nov. 17, 1896, and Michelet's *La Sorcière* (Bruxelles and Leipzig: A. Lacroix, Verboeckhoven, 1863), Widener Library, Harvard. For the interpretation of Wier and Mejer, see James's copy of Snell, especially references in the pencilled index on the last two blank pages of the book (note 9 above); and Wier's *De Praestigiis Daemonum,* 1563.

21. See James's marks in Snell, 69.

22. See Calmeil, *De la Folie,* II, 49, and Baissac, *Les Grands jours,* 541, which James's 1896 lecture notes cite.

23. For a translation of Spee's *Cautio,* see A. C. Kors and E. Peters, eds., *Witchcraft in Europe* (Philadelphia: University of Pennsylvania Press, 1972), 351. For a sketch of Phillip Schönborn, see *Allgemeine Deutsche Biographie* (Berlin: Duncker & Humblot, 1971), vol. 32, 274–276 (reprinted from 1891).

LECTURE VII: *DEGENERATION*

1. The full quotation is taken from James's "The Dilemma of Determinism," in *The Will to Believe,* 153.

2. From James's *Talks to Teachers on Psychology* (New York: Holt, 1899), 164. This is a good example of how a scattered section of James's published prose corresponds exactly to a portion of his unpublished lecture notes on Exceptional Mental States.

3. See Charles E. Rosenberg, *The Trial of the Assassin Guiteau* (Chicago: University of Chicago Press, 1968).

4. Morel's classic work, *Traité des dégénérescences physiques, intellectuelles et morales de l'espèce humaine et des causes qui produisent ces variétés maladives,* first published in 1857, was well known to James, who checked the text and accompanying atlas out of the library for his graduate lectures on mental pathology in the early 1890s. At the same time, James read the work of other Degeneration theorists—such as Magnan, Moreau (de Tours), Legrain, Voisin, Noir, Séglas, Laurent, and Falret in France; Krafft-Ebing, Koch, and Schramm in Germany; Lombroso in Italy; Nisbet and Maudsley in England; and Régis and MacDonald in America —extensively. See the Library Charging Records, Harvard Archives, and the discussion in Ellenberger, *Discovery of the Unconscious,* 281; also F. Alexander and S. Salesnik, *The History of Psychiatry* (New York: Harper & Row, 1966).

5. In 1878, James reviewed R. L. Dugdale's *The Jukes: A Study in Crime, Pauperism, Disease, and Heredity* in *Atlantic Monthly,* 41 (March 1878), 405, as a scientifically oriented alternative to the Degeneracy theory. Dugdale had examined the social damage done by 1,200 members of the same family suffering from pauperism, crime, disease, and mental problems, and estimated that it had cost more than $125 million over the generations studied for society to prosecute, maintain in prison and poorhouse, supply with drugs, cover the cost of damage done, and invest time in this family—to no avail. While hereditary disease certainly played a major role, Dugdale clearly implicated the environment in the final shaping of each character.

6. The extra set of notes for the "Degeneration" lecture, Houghton Library, Harvard, corresponds in even greater detail to the outline of ideas presented in the original set of lecture notes. For a brief review of the concept of neurasthenia, see E. T. Carlson, "George Miller Beard and Neurasthenia," in Wallace and Pressley, *Essays in the History of Psychiatry,* 50.

7. List of the most highly prized books and pamphlets in

James's library, in the hand of Alice Howe Gibbens James, James Papers, Houghton Library, Harvard.

8. James's copy, containing marginal marks and a penciled index, was given to the Harvard College Library by his wife sometime after James's death. The example in question is on "page 30," along with James's penciled marks in the margin. See H. Kaan, *Der neurasthenische Angstaffect bei Zwangsvorstellungen, und der Primordiale Grübelzwang* (Leipzig and Vienna: Franz Deuticke, 1893), Houghton Library, containing James's marginal marks and pencilled index.

9. Magnan had made significant contributions to the pathology of the central nervous system before turning his attention to the problems of epilepsy, delirium, the impulsions, and the effects of various substances such as cocaine, ether, and alcohol on consciousness. Eugen Bleuler, C. G. Jung's teacher, had been a student of both Charcot and Magnan.

10. V. Magnan, *Recherche sur les centres nerveux, alcoholisme, folie des héréditaires dégenérés, paralysie générale, médecine légale,* 2nd series (Paris: Masson, 1893).

11. Ibid., 283.

12. Kaan, *Der neurasthenische Angstaffect,* 117; cf. note 8.

13. Magnan, *Recherche sur les centres nerveux,* 285.

14. James, "Is Life Worth Living?" in *The Will to Believe,* 39.

15. Throughout his career, James had countered Kant's philosophy with his own interpretation of empiricism, beginning with his first reading of Kant in the late 1860s while in dialogue with Oliver Wendell Holmes, Jr. In addition, Charles Sanders Peirce, an early influence on James, was an expert on Kant; but it was not the revision of Kant's categories that most attracted James to Peirce's philosophy. Nor did James agree with Schopenhauer and Hegel, both of whom derived from Kant. Kant, according to James, had an unwarranted penchant for declaring that life could be known only in terms of absolutes, and James thought him guilty

of "circuitous and ponderous artifices." James patently objected to Kant's "mythical machine shop of forms and categories to which everything metaphysical and psychological must be referred." See various references to James's interpretation of Kant in R. B. Perry's *Thought and Character of William James,* and James's various notes and unpublished essays on Kant in the James Papers, Houghton Library, Harvard.

16. "How is nature possible" comes from James's notes of 1868, 13–16, found by Perry between the leaves of James's text on Kant used in the 1896 Psychological Seminary at Harvard. See also the translation of Kant's *Classification of Mental Disorders* by Charles T. Sullivan (Doylestown, Pa.: The Doylestown Foundation, 1964).

17. James was well read in the current literature of neurology, brain physiology, and the most recent psychiatric advances in France, Germany, Italy, England, and America. He had read Ferrier, DuBois-Reymond, Ziehen, Exner, Bucknell and Tuke, Esquirol and Pinel, Clouston, Maudsley, Griesinger, Spizka, and Krafft-Ebing, among others. And through Adolf Meyer, then at Worcester State Hospital, he was familiar with the newest classification of mental illness proposed by Emil Kraeplin. See Harvard College Library Charging Records, 1889 to 1896, University Archives, by permission.

Adolf Meyer had produced a typescript, abridged translation of Emil Kraeplin's *Psychiatry* by 1901, which circulated in the Boston scene. Some of Meyer's assistants, among them August Hoch, has been to Europe to study with Kraeplin and learn his classification schemes. By far the most scientific of the day, Kraeplin's system was brought back to Boston just before 1900. A copy of Meyer's translation and condensation of Kraeplin is on deposit at Rare Books, Francis A. Countway Library of Medicine, Harvard.

18. See James on Morselli's *Manuale della Semejotica delle Malattie Mentali* in *Psychological Review,* 3 (1896), 679–681.

19. Cowles, an active Boston psychotherapist, taught courses on mental disease at the Medical School during the same period in which James taught his graduate course in mental pathology at Harvard College. Cowles referred to James extensively in his lectures, and James had read closely Cowles's recent book *Neurasthenia* and his essay on the mechanisms of insanity. James had taken his students on field trips to McLean, and it was probably Cowles who arranged for James to stay at McLean under an assumed name while being treated for depression. See Edward Cowles, Faculty Records, Rare Books, Francis A. Countway Library of Medicine, Harvard, by permission; Cowles's *Neurasthenia,* with James's extensive marks, Houghton Library, Harvard; and Cowles's "Introductory Lectures on Principles of Mental Pathology and the Nature of Mental Symptoms, Revised to 1903," Rare Books, Francis A. Countway Library of Medicine, Harvard; by permission. The controversial problem of James's dates in attendance at McLean involves records that are restricted by the literary executors of the James Estate.

20. See minutes of the 25th meeting of the Boston Medico-Psychological Society, Jan. 22, 1885, Rare Books, Francis A. Countway Library of Medicine, Harvard.

21. See *American Journal of Insanity,* 240, for 1896; also 1892 and 1850 for possible references.

22. Ibid., 1850, 240.

23. Henri Legrand du Saulle, physician at the Bicêtre (sister asylum to the Salpêtrière), was known for his contributions to the study of general paralysis, epilepsy, and to the field of medical jurisprudence.

24. H. Legrand du Saulle, *La Folie du doute avec délire du toucher* (Paris: Adrien Delahaye, 1875), 35–36.

25. Van Eeden, a Dutch physician and pioneer in the modern psychotherapy of the subconscious, was also known as a poet. He had studied briefly in Nancy with Bernheim, and on his return to Holland in 1887 organized the first clinic for the practice of suggestive therapeutics with a col-

league, Van Roentergam. He described the work of this clinic at the International Congress of Experimental Psychology in Paris in August 1889, which James and the young Freud, along with Azam, Babinski, Binet, Delboeuf, Dessoir, Lombroso, and others, all attended.

26. The example James cited for his 1896 audience was first communicated by Van Eeden at the winter meeting of the Society for Psychiatry at Utrecht in November 1890, and subsequently published in the *Revue de l'hypnotisme* in 1892. The set of these journals that belonged to James, now in the Widener Library, contains James's marginal marks, and the citation in James's notes is to the case described by Van Eeden.

27. F. Van Eeden, "Les Obsessions," *Revue de l'hypnotisme* (1892), WJ's copy, Widener Library, Harvard.

28. James's detailed notes cite an example from the work of Dr. P. Brémaud, chief physician of the French Navy and professor at the School of Naval Medicine at Brest. Brémaud had published work on various cases of attempted suicide treated at the Naval Hospital, specifying the kind of psychotherapeutic treatment applied in each instance. James cited Brémaud's assessment of a patient who had attempted suicide eight times. See P. Brémaud, "Observation d'un hystérique," *Revue de l'hypnotisme* (1893), 292, WJ's copy.

29. The dissertation was *Du Fractionnement des opérations cérébrales et en particulier de leur dédoublement dans les psychopathies* (Paris: A. Parent, 1882). James owned a special edition of Descourtis's work, which was given to Harvard College by Mrs. William James in 1921. But James also checked out of the Harvard College Library another copy, which he marked up and used for his lecture. The bookplate shows that this particular volume came into the library on February 6, 1890, and, according to the Charging Records, James checked it out immediately. The original date due stamp is still in the back, and it contains the dates James checked the book out throughout the 1890s, corresponding to

the dates in the Charging Records. Harvard College Library copies; see also the Harvard College Library Charging Records for 1889–90.

30. Originally enunciated in 1833, J. C. Prichard's most complete statement on moral insanity came in 1835 with the publication of his *Treatise on Insanity and Other Diseases Affecting the Mind* (Philadelphia: Carey & Hart, 1837). The 1837 edition in the Harvard College Library contains a few of James's marginal marks.

31. Prichard, *Treatise on Insanity*, Widener Library, Harvard. See also the Library Charging Records, Harvard Archives.

32. For James's relation to Münsterberg, see Perry's *Thought and Character of William James*; M. Münsterberg, *Hugo Münsterberg: His Life and Work* (New York: Appleton, 1922). See H. Münsterberg, *Psychotherapy* (New York: Moffat & Yard, 1909) for cases.

33. See G. Danville, *La Psychologie de l'amour,* Rare Books, Francis A. Countway Library of Medicine, Boston, for what looks like James's marginal marks. See also the Harvard Library Charging Records for 1895 as the date when James checked the book out; Harvard Archives, by permission.

LECTURE VIII: *GENIUS*

1. Adapted from "Genius not a Disease; Lecture by Prof. James in the course on 'Exceptional Mental States,' " *Boston Herald,* Nov. 15, 1896, 9. Lady Somerset was the wife of Lord Henry Somerset who was leader of the temperance movement in England.

2. This and other major portions of Lecture VIII are abstracted from James's alternate set of lecture notes marked "Genius and Insanity," James Papers, Houghton Library, Harvard.

3. See Myers, "The Subliminal Consciousness; The "Mechanism of Genius," *Proceedings of the English Society for Psychical Research,* 8 (1892), 333–361, and his *Human Personality and Its Survival of Bodily Death* (New York: Longmans, Green, 1907).

4. The French psychiatrist L.-F. Lélut distinguished himself by his extensive investigations in phrenology, which he followed by studies of the effects on memory of sleep deprivation and confinement. In 1846 he published an analysis of the so-called "hallucinations" of Pascal, and in 1856 he attempted to apply current psychological theories to an analysis of Socrates in his *Du Démon de Socrate: Spécimén d'une application de la science psychologique à celle de l'histoire* (Paris: Baillière, 1836). James had read both these works.

Jacques-Joseph Moreau (of Tours) also contributed to Degeneracy theory, principally through his book *La Psychologie morbide* (1859). Moreau believed that the world of the mentally ill was more like a dream world than the world of normal people. Morbidity, he said, was marked by diminishing intellectual functions and the inflation of unusually insignificant psychic contents. Moreau's theory of *désagrégation*—the separating of psychic functions from conscious control—had an important influence on Pierre Janet and predated the Freudian idea of repression by more than twenty-five years. Moreau was best known for his studies of degeneration and genius, however.

Cesare Lombroso, the Italian criminologist and professor of psychiatry at the University of Turin, was one of the founders of criminal anthropology. He wrote on a wide range of topics, but particularly on the relation between insanity and genius. Originally developed in an 1864 essay while still a young medical student, his *Entartung und Genie (Genius and Insanity),* first published in German, became a full-length book that had gone into six editions by 1894. Following Moreau, Lombroso made extensive studies on the prevalence of insanity in families of genius.

John Ferguson Nisbet was an English doctor, who in his *Insanity of Genius* took Lombroso's ideas on genius and insanity to the extreme by concluding that every unusual personality was insane.

5. See the Library Charging Records, Harvard Archives, for James's extensive reading of these authors between 1889 and 1896; James's article on "Degeneration and Genius," *Psychological Review*, 2 (1895), 287–294; his essay on "Great Men and Their Environment" in *The Will to Believe* (originally published in a longer version in *Atlantic Monthly*, 46 [1880], 441–459); and references to genius in the *Varieties*, particularly the first chapter on Religion and Neurology. Other sources, aside from the *Principles*, include James's speech on "The True Harvard," *Harvard Graduates' Magazine*, 12 (1903), 5–8; his "Stanford's Ideal Destiny," *Leland Stanford Junior University Publications*, 14 (1906), 5–8; and "The Social Value of the College Bred," *McClure's Magazine*, 30 (1908), 419–422.

6. Lélut, *Du Démon de Socrate*.

7. For a summary of James's opinion of the hallucination question, see his essay "What Psychical Research Has Accomplished," in *The Will to Believe*.

8. J.-J. Moreau, *La Psychologie morbide dans ses rapports avec la philosophie de l'histoire et de l'influence des névropathies sur le dynamisme intellectuel* (Paris: Victor Masson, 1859), Houghton Library, Harvard.

9. Ibid., 560–561 of James's copy.

10. References to Lombroso taken from the English translation of his *Man of Genius* (London: Walter Scott, 1891). James reviewed Lombroso's 1894 edition of this work, *Entartung und Genie*, in 1895. The references to Lombroso in the present 1896 lectures suggest that James cited Lombroso from memory and could not remember the exact date of the publication he was referring to.

11. J. F. Nisbet, *The Insanity of Genius and the General Inequality of the Human Faculty Physiologically Considered* (London: Ward & Downey, 1891). James's lecture notes cite page xv. The Harvard College Library copy was checked out by James throughout the 1890s.

12. Ibid.

13. James summarizes these authors again in the *Varieties,* 16–17.

14. Adapted from James's article on the "Degeneration and Genius" authors, *Psychological Review,* 1895, 289. A comparison of the Exceptional Mental States lecture notes of 1896 and the "Degeneration and Genius" review of 1895 shows that James lifted the same ideas and probably whole passages out of the 1895 piece for the 1896 lectures.

15. Alternate set of lecture notes marked "Genius and Insanity," 20, cites p. 315 in Nisbet's *Insanity of Genius.*

16. James continued his critique of Nordau in the *Varieties,* where he said: "Nordau seeks to undermine all mysticism by exposing the weakness of the lower kinds. Mysticism for him means any sudden perception of hidden significance in things. He explains such perceptions by the abundant uncompleted associations which experiences may arouse in a degenerate brain. These give to him who has the experience a vague and vast sense of its leading further, yet they awaken no definite or useful consequent in his thought. The explanation is a plausible one for certain sorts of feeling of significance; and other alienists (Wernicke, for example, in his *Grundriss der Psychiatrie,* 1896) have explained 'paranoic' conditions by a laming of the association-organ. But the higher mystical flights, with their positiveness and abruptness, are surely products of no such merely negative condition. It seems far more reasonable to ascribe them to inroads from the subconscious life, or the cerebral activity correlative of which we as yet know nothing" — 427.

17. Text is drawn from the original 1896 lecture notes, while the conclusion comes from a crossed-out line in the

alternate set of lecture notes on "Genius and Insanity," page 16.

18. This passage conforms to the abbreviations in James's original 1896 lecture notes; it is repeated again in more detail in the alternate set of lecture notes on "Genius and Insanity," and it is written out in readable text in James's 1895 review of the "Degeneration and Genius" authors, 291–292.

19. James's 1896 lecture notes cite Nisbet's "proof of nervous disease to all disease 3½ times in geniuses than in the g'nl popn." The alternate set of lecture notes on "Genius and Insanity" gives this idea as a literary ratio; but the 1895 review of the "Degeneration and Genius" authors gives a completely readable text of these ideas in one of James's long footnotes, page 295.

20. "Degeneration and Genius" review, 295.

21. Ibid.

22. The original 1896 notes refer briefly to Emerson, Holmes, Longfellow, and Whittier. The fully written out text referring to these men appears in the 1895 "Degeneration and Genius" review, 293.

23. James, "Great Men, Great Thoughts, and Their Environment," *Atlantic Monthly*, 46 (1880), 453–454. The alternate set of lecture notes refers to "Boston list, Lowell, OWH, Longfellow, Emerson."

24. "Degeneration and Genius" review, 293, which compares to the list of names in the alternate set of lecture notes, and the original 1896 lecture notes.

25. The first part of this paragraph conforms to the exact phrases in the 1896 lecture notes. The remainder is made up of the phrases in the 1896 notes, but expanded more fully in the 1895 "Degeneration and Genius" review, 295.

26. James's references to Bain here are important, first because of Bain's association with Henry James, Sr., through Thomas Carlyle's literary circle in England between 1844 and 1856; and second, because of the influence of Bain's ideas on the formation of pragmatism as an American phi-

losophical movement, which, according to C. S. Peirce, began at meetings of the Cambridge Metaphysical Club held alternately at James's house and Peirce's in the early 1870s. In the *Principles,* James had made extensive use of Bain, especially his conception of analysis and intuition as different cognitive styles. See "Alexander Bain," *Encyclopaedia Britannica,* vol. 3 (New York: Cambridge University Press, 1910), 11th ed., 221; also Bain's *John Stuart Mill: A Criticism, with Personal Recollections* (London: Longmans, Green, 1882); and Bain's *Autobiography* (New York: Longmans, Green, 1904). See also Max Fisch, "Was There a Cambridge Metaphysical Club?" in E. C. Moore and R. S. Robin, *Studies in the Philosophy of Charles Sanders Peirce,* 2nd series (Amherst, Mass.: University of Massachusetts Press, 1961), 3–32.

27. *Principles,* I, 530; see also *Varieties,* 23f.

28. James, "Great Men, Great Thoughts, and Their Environment," op. cit., 456.

29. James's 1896 lecture notes say "first class originality of intellect! Bain has analyzed that. . . ." I have given here the more well developed version from his alternate set of lecture notes on "Genius and Insanity," 22.

30. The 1896 lecture notes follow closely this passage from the alternate set of lecture notes on "Genius and Insanity," 22. James repeats these ideas in more detail in his chapter on Religion and Neurology in the *Varieties.*

31. James developed this idea further in the *Varieties* when he said: "Borderland insanity, crankiness, insane temperament, loss of mental balance, psychic degeneration, to use a few of the many synonyms by which [genius] has been called, has certain peculiarities which, when combined with a superior quality of intellect in an individual, make it more probable that he will make his mark and affect his age, than if his temperament were less neurotic. There is of course no special affinity between crankiness as such and superior intellect, for most psychopaths have feeble intellects, and superior intellects more commonly have normal nervous

systems. But the psychopathic temperament, whatever be the intellect with which it finds itself paired, often brings with it ardor and excitability of character. The cranky person has extraordinary emotional susceptibility. He is liable to fixed ideas and obsessions. His conceptions tend to pass immediately into belief and action; and when he gets a new idea, he has no rest until he proclaims it, or in some way 'works it off' "— 22–23.

32. I have followed here the original 1896 set of lecture notes, but added related material from the alternate set of notes on "Genius and Insanity," 21.

33. C. S. Peirce Papers, Houghton Library, Harvard; original typescript translation; and Peirce's correspondence with Appleton; courtesy of Max Fisch. Peirce had begun correspondence with Appleton & Company early in 1895 concerning the translation of Hirsch's book; that same year James reviewed the German edition favorably in *Psychological Review*, suggesting again the extent to which Peirce and James exerted an influence on each other. Peirce, hoping to complete the work in four easy installments, had to do the translating in New York. Problems arose over reading the page proofs, and the translation was delayed and almost canceled for a time; it appeared finally in 1896. Peirce then wrote a review of his own English translation in which he emphasized that Hirsch argued for environmental influences over against the theories of Lombroso and Nordau.

Throughout the 1880s and early 1890s Peirce had written extensively on the nature of genius, particularly among eighteenth- and nineteenth-century American men of science. He essentially agreed with James's position that the greatest of men are the most human of human beings, despite appearances. In fact, much of James's focus on the mind of the genius parallels that of Peirce. James's discussions began in his "Great Men, Great Thoughts, and Their Environment" (1880). Then followed several papers in which he argued with

Grant Allen over the theory of Social Darwinism. "The Importance of Individuals" (1892) was the sequel to the essay on great men. James also discussed genius in the *Principles*, drawing heavily on Alexander Bain; and finally, in 1895, he reviewed the "Degeneration and Genius" authors, Jules Dallemagne, Lombroso, Nordau, Nisbet, and Hirsch. Most of Peirce's studies of genius occurred during this same period.

Although James considered Peirce himself something of an eccentric genius, Peirce, despite all his flaws, was the recipient of James's aid on several occasions. In 1902, for instance, James wrote the Carnegie Fund in support of a grant for Peirce. When John Shaw Billings responded with inquiries, James wrote back on June 28 that, should the grant be awarded, he hoped the Fund would exert on Peirce a severe constraint as to deadlines, since that would help Peirce order himself considerably. "Your institute," James continued, "will be collecting endless material for a future book on 'the tragedy of genius'—especially that of semi-genius. Peirce is a tragic personality, but his is a *real* genius, of a discontinuous kind, and with all his arbitrariness, [there is] a very lovable side to his character. I never knew a human being like him." See William James to John Shaw Billings, June 28, 1902, James Folder, Archives, New York Public Library.

34. See Peirce's unpublished book review of Hirsch's *Genius and Degeneration*, Peirce Papers, Houghton Library, Harvard. Also the catalogue to the Peirce Papers, Reading Room, Houghton Library, Harvard, 131–132, for parallels with James's statements on genius.

35. See James's copy of Hirsch, *Genie und Entartung* (Berlin: Oscar C. Coblentz, 1894), with WJ's autograph, address, and marginal marks.

36. Adapted from James's *Talks to Teachers on Psychology*, 113, which follows exactly the ideas of the 1896 lecture notes. See also his 1895 article on the "Degeneration and Genius" authors, 294.

37. Adapted from James's 1895 article on the "Degeneration and Genius" authors, *Psychological Review*, 294, and the 1896 notes.

38. Ibid., and *Varieties*, 25.

39. Compare the 1896 lecture notes here with the conclusion to James's essay "Is Life Worth Living?" and the conclusion to his 1895 "Degeneration and Genius" article.

40. Final lines from the 1896 lecture notes, with slight modifications for grammatical style.

INDEX

St. Vitus' dance, 114. *See also*
  imitative chorea
Salem witchcraft, 6, 111–12,
  124, 125–26, 127
Samoa, 95
Saulle, Henri Legrand du, 143–44
Schander, Ilma, 16
Schönborn, Johann Phillip von,
  129
Schmidkunz, Hans, 26n
Schrenck-Notzing, Dr. Albert von,
  39
science, relationship between
  religion and, 1–2
scientific psychology, 1–2
secondary intelligent consciousness, 39–41, 43–44, 52
  subliminal consciousness and,
  41–42
secondary mnemonic (memory)
  chains, 87
sedentary life, diseases of, 158–59
self-consciousness, 39
sense stimuli, dreams and, 27–29
sensory motor channels, messages
  from. *See* automatism
sexual exhaustion, theory of
  neurosis, 13
shamming, hysteria and, 58–59
Sidis, Boris, 13
sight, temporary loss of, 79
skin, hysteria and, 56, 62
sleep
  attitude toward, 15–16
  comparison of natural and
    hypnotically induced, 31
  hypnogogic imagery induced
    during, 27–29
  pathological, 16
  "post-effects" of, 33
  protracted, 77, 78
  suggestion of waking at given
    time, 31
  tactile sensibility in, 175n
"sleep-drunkenness"

overemphasis on single idea
  during, 19–21
similarity to dreaming, 20–21
smell, hysteria and, 54, 70
Snell, Dr. Otto, 116, 125
Social Darwinism, 1, 11
social reform, fixed ideas and,
  147–48
Socrates, 151, 203n
somnambulism, 20–21
  definition of, 22
  dream imagery and patients
    prone to, 29–30
  multiple personality and, 74,
    84, 86
  See also "natural somnambul-
    ism"
spectral evidence, 121
spirits. *See* mediumship
splitting, 41
  hysteria and, 63–65
  weakness and, 85
spontaneous drawing, 49
Sprenger, James, 115
"stigmata," of mentally ill, 132
stream of consciousness, suggestibility and, 26–27
subconscious
  dual powers of, 43n
  and incapacity to fix attention,
    22
  traumatic shock and, 64
  uniqueness of, 12–13
subconscious fixed ideas, hysteria
  and, 69–71
subconscious intelligence, 44
subconscious memory, 44
"sub-cortical centers," 40
subliminal, 11–12
  automatic writing and, 49–52
  collective irrational impulses
    of, 123
  evidence for, 53
  exorcism and, 128
  genius and, 149–50